PIERCING THE LION HEART

PIERCING THE LION HEART

The True Crime Story of the
Betrayal and Murder of
Undercover Cop Jimmy Hoff

J. Andre Boles & Ron Hutcherson

To the memory of all the cops who gave their lives in the line of duty

CONTENTS

BOOK ONE – DOIN' THE DEAL

Book Two – Nevada Justice

BOOK ONE

DOIN' THE DEAL

Chapter 1

DEAD OR ALIVE?

Jimmy Hoff stood at the edge of the riverbank looking down the slope into the darkness before him. The trees along the river had thinned out and only the brush that tugged at his pant legs grew in the low spot. He hesitated, trying to pick up movement or a rustle of sound. He heard only the gurgle of the translucent river that lay before him.

The quiet darkness raised his hackles; it was too quiet, too still. Eyes squinted he cocked his head to the side in a futile attempt to see into the dark shadows. On this moonless night, it was particularly dark along the Truckee River. Willows and cottonwoods grew thick along the river just west of downtown Reno. Reno Police Undercover Officer Jimmy Hoff had followed 20-year-old Edward "Tom" Wilson to this spot and was now considering his options.

Jimmy, who had started his police career as a military policeman after two hitches as an M.P. in the army, joined the Reno Police Department in 1971. Soon after hitting the brightly lit, casino-lined streets of the "Biggest Little City," he became a K-9 officer partnered up with a German Shepherd named Judge. The dog liked cheese and, like his master, catching crooks. Although Jimmy and Judge won many medals at canine contests in Nevada and California, Judge was far more than a well-trained performer. He was Jimmy's best friend and partner.

One night Jimmy and Judge responded to a fight call on South Virginia Street, Reno's main drag. There Jimmy encountered three rowdies ready to rock and roll with the solo officer. Judge was waiting in the black and white for the beckoning call. When the fighters turned their anger on the cop, he whistled and the dog came out and put those three potential assailants up against the wall.

Jimmy would not remain a K-9 officer. He was devastated one day when he came in and found Judge lying lifeless on the floor. His canine partner was dead. Jimmy cried for three days.

As the heartbreak lessened, Jimmy searched for a replacement. He found a younger dog and began the intensive training needed to put him on the street. As the dog grew into its role as the cop's new partner, one leg went bad. Jimmy found a vet who offered to fix the problem. Jimmy set his mind to save his dog's career but the cost of corrective surgery was prohibitive. The RPD budget wouldn't cover it.

Jimmy didn't want to get rid of the dog. The K-9 Unit held a meeting and, in a heated discussion, he was told that the dog wasn't up for the job. Jimmy resisted but finally agreed. Jimmy and the dog would both leave the unit. A little later he left K-9. He kept the dog at the cost of his role on the team.

As a seasoned officer with numerous commendations from both citizens and supervisors, Jimmy was welcome to work where he wanted. "Jimmy was a good officer, a good guy all the way around," one of Jimmy's human partners said. "He was a very easy-going guy when the pressure wasn't on, but in a tight situation he was very focused—all business. He had an ego, but it wasn't out of control. I saw him drop some guys, but it was part of the job. We were there to enforce the laws. If we ran into resistance, the scale would go up. We got the best calls, the bad ones. Hell, that's what we were there for. Sometimes people would overreact (be critical), but I never saw Jimmy brutalize anybody or go over the line."

Jimmy's reputation earned him a berth in the RPD's narcotics squad. He closeted his blue and gold uniform and switched to the casual dress of an undercover narcotics officer. It was a good fit. He had a natural. laid-back demeanor and pleasant personality. If he came into a room, you'd know he was there but it wouldn't be because he was talking. That would serve him well on the job.

It quickly became apparent that Jimmy could buy dope, and the fact is that few cops can do that. Lured by the prospect of keen rushes built on living on the edge, they get into what they see as the ultimate game. Most, however, don't play it very well. Some are lousy actors, wooden and stiff, as if "narc" had been etched into their foreheads. Some can't slide into the role of a street person. Some need supervision, that shift-by-shift regimentation, to keep them focused. Others are too slow in the head, or too methodical. Some find that they're just too scared to walk lightly—and most often alone—in a world of dopers and street people.

Some start out okay, but with time and association they not only blend with, but emulate, their targets. They take a hit or two to prove they're not "the man" but soon they become what they hunt. They've been snared by the trap they set out to disable. It's a known hazard, and in 1979 the general practice in the RPD was to limit a tour as an undercover narc to eighteen months. Most, in that time, didn't get infected.

Jimmy had none of those problems. He had developed a reputation as a good cop who stayed alert and could read people. He was so good that he was allowed to stay on in narcotics. He liked the work. He was comfortable and the owner of eyes that invited confidence.

His job was to find, deal with and jail drug dealers. His tools included disguise, deception and lots of nerve. He quickly compiled an impressive arrest record. It is well documented that 20 percent of street cops make 80 percent of the arrests that result in felony convictions. Jimmy belonged to the 20 percent club.

"Jimmy was on a run," Detective Frank Torres, who worked closely with Jimmy, later recalled. "He was starting to get a little cocky…I'm sure he felt invincible and thought he could do everything."

Even so, Jimmy had decided that this was his last buy. He had been in narcotics for two and a half years—perhaps too long—and he planned to rotate back to an assignment in uniform. But he wanted to go out with a last big buy, and any narc who could boast of having bought anything close to a pound in a hand-to-hand transaction was a heavy. Sixteen ounces of powder—heroin, speed or cocaine—stood out as a benchmark for recognition as a hard-hitting undercover agent. This bust would be Jimmy's trophy.

The 32-year-old, still in his physical prime, was tough as rawhide and knew no fear as he followed Wilson's barely discernable black silhouette toward the river and the alleged location of a stash of ten ounces of cocaine. That amount of high quality coke was worth 16,000 dollars. That was wholesale price. Jimmy, highly disciplined both physically and mentally, stood nearly six feet and weighed in at a trim 180 pounds. Wilson, the purported cocaine salesman who was just as ready to go mano-a-mano, stood a bit taller and shared the same slim athletic build.

They were headed through the brush and trees toward the riverbank where Wilson was to retrieve the goods. The cash was in the car, Jimmy's "pimp ride" that was actually Jimmy's girlfriend Kitty's car, a shiny new 280ZX with two seats and a hard top that ran like a bullet. Jimmy's private vehicle was a pickup truck, a green four-wheel drive '72. Fellow officers knew he regarded it as his pride and joy, but it didn't fit the image of Jimmy as drug dealer, Jimmy the pimp. He left it parked and borrowed the 280ZX to use in narcotics transactions because it made him look like the real thing, a heavy buyer. It happened to be the fastest car in use by the police department, either marked or unmarked. Neither the RPD nor anyone in Narcotics or Vice had wheels that could stay with, catch or overtake that 280ZX in surveillance or pursuit.

While Jimmy stood scoping out the path ahead of him, 18-year-old John "Steve" Olausen held his breath and prayed that he not be spotted. He lay on the cool earth near the end of the inclined path covered with branches that he and his two hidden cohorts had cut earlier. The three made not a move as they listened to Wilson approach with Jimmy in tow. Jimmy the narc expertly played his role as pimp and dope dealer. The pair walked the dirt path, footfall after footfall. There was soft chatter between the two. It was impossible to see them, but their voices told the teenagers that Wilson was approaching with the target. They waited in their blinds. Time slowed down. Each one tried to suppress his breathing to avoid any whisper of sound. It became a game to them, a game played by deadly men children.

Wilson walked past Olausen down the meandering path, frequented largely by brush bunnies and the occasional brash coyote, giving a quick glance toward his concealed accomplice. Poised at the edge of what was about to become the crime scene, Jimmy let out a breath and in a low voice told himself, "This looks like a setup."

Close enough to hear the softly spoken words, Olausen tensed. In his right hand, he held an open Buck knife. It was not a run-of-the-mill folding knife. The heavy stainless steel three-and-a-half-inch blade was long enough to penetrate the heart of a normal size man, strong enough to cut through a steel bolt and was honed to a razor's edge. Olausen had for some time owned the weapon which he could open with the flick of a wrist, but he was not experienced in the art of actual knife combat. This night it would ultimately not matter.

While Jimmy stood at the precipice looking downward, Olausen could feel his pulse pounding in his ears. When the undercover cop padded softly past Olausen, the ambush stalled. Olausen held his breath and froze. Jimmy remained unharmed.

Once past the hesitant Olausen, Jimmy continued to follow Wilson toward the river. The night air had turned electric. Olausen and the two other armed boys shook with fear and anticipation as they huddled on the ground beneath freshly-cut brush. While Olausen clutched the Buck knife, the other two ambushers held freshly sharpened butcher knives from a professional chef's set. Jimmy might have seen the glint from one of the gleaming blades had there been significant light.

Buyer and seller walked toward the site of an abandoned pump house where Wilson had concealed the merchandise, past the two other strategically placed blinds. The youngest occupant, 16-year-old David Lani, crouched down in the bushes, holding the long blade in front of his right thigh. His fear of Jimmy turned the spring in his legs to gelatin. As they neared the third accomplice, Fred Stites, he, like the others, froze.

Jimmy did not feel the intensity the boys did. He'd been there before, making a buy, waiting for the bust, knowing he had backup. Wilson, barely into adulthood, should be easy to handle. He might have an accomplice. Still, Wilson and his pal, who the snitch, Anne Marie, had already identified, were hardly more than kids. They were not known to have weapons. Certainly Anne Marie, would have warned Jimmy if she knew that Wilson and Olausen went about armed. Jimmy was confident and his cover officers were more confident. Confident enough for them to drop their guard—to drop the guard that could keep Jimmy alive.

In all the buy/bust or let-the-money-walk operations, the safety of the undercover agent is paramount. The greatest sin is running an undercover drug buyer into a rip-off where he or she is without sufficient protection. In early 1979, the narcotics detail in the RPD's Detective Division and Jimmy's backup was comprised of Sgt. Brown, Jimmy Hoff, John (J.D.) Douglas, Gary Eubanks and Randy Flocchini. Jimmy told his family that Flocchini was his best friend and Eubanks a "real good friend."

Douglas, a black officer and an Air Guardsman, had a tongue sharp enough to start a Gillette factory, and he backed it with enough brass for a foundry. "He was very articulate and very bright," Jimmy's stepbrother Dennis said later. Douglas was the standout in his crowd, known for his fast talk and quick wit. He wasn't big, but his mouth made up for a lack of physical presence. He acted tough, he talked tough, and it worked—whether truth or bluff. One veteran described him as having a "bulldog mouth and a hound dog ass."

Gary Eubanks came on as the opposite of Douglas. His tall and extremely thin frame, coupled with a noticeably aloof stare, earned him the name "Whip" in the RPD. In 1979, he was still a youngster, not much older than the boys plotting to do Jimmy in. He had a reputation in the department for prowess in martial arts, but the perception was that he didn't really like to scrap. Still, despite his reputation, height and arrogance, Eubanks had a detracting feature—his gait. He walked like a duck. His splay-footed carriage made him seem surprisingly awkward.

What Eubanks lacked in actual physical and mental toughness, he made up for in cockiness—earned or not. He made it a habit in narcotics to wear the beard and long hair of a user, set off by another mark of the drug world dandy, a black Italian leather jacket. He'd come to the RPD as a teenage cadet, and the department would be the only employer he would ever have. As a cadet, he curried favor with supervisors and reserved his arrogance for those who came after him and remained his subordinates in seniority, rank or assignment. Only to those above him did he manifest politeness bordering on servility, taking pains to make known his willingness to work hard and put in long hours. However, Whip's standing was to be blemished. What not everyone in the RPD knew at the time, and those who did know chose to overlook, was that he was a drug user.

Regardless, the team usually functioned flawlessly. Until this night.

The buy/bust should have been routine: get the stuff, pull the gun, flash the gold star, and make the arrest, with or without backup. But tonight, Officer Hoff, who was well taught and experienced in all sorts of combat skills including firearms, was not packing heat. He was without the short-barreled, .38 caliber, heavy steel revolver loaded with six hollow point rounds that turned a man's guts into hamburger, having left both his gun and the body wire in the car in order to carry out this charade.

The body wire, a broadcasting unit about the size of a deck of cards, figured heavily in officer safety in Reno in 1979. The usual procedure was to tape it to the officer's lower abdomen just under the belt, making it unlikely to be discovered. In ordinary use, the wearer taped a small microphone to his chest and a thin wire about two feet long ran down the torso to the broadcasting unit. The mike would pick up the voice of the wearer and, under ideal conditions, the voice of others nearby.

The transmitter part of the device allowed cover officers to stay a reasonable distance away from the buyer and still listen to and record any dialog between the buyer and dope dealer. Generally, the device was reliable for picking up the utterances of the wearer, and could alert team members about any trouble as well as whether and when they needed to move in. Going in solo without a wire was downright reckless.

It was equally foolhardy to proceed unarmed.

Perhaps Jimmy's decisions were the product of his misplaced trust in the cover officers, Sergeant "Downtown" Brown and his team. Either way, he walked into the brush alone, unarmed and without the one-way communication device that could keep his team in the loop.

Jimmy, who had decided not even to carry his detective badge, watched the younger man moving ahead of him.

"It's right here," Wilson said in a loud voice, his heart rate accelerating as they approached the riverbank.

As Jimmy looked at Wilson's back, the cop did not see the would-be assassins concealed nearby, holding a couple of feet of cold steel intended for the buyer of cocaine. Neither did Hoff's backup officers, who had not tailed him closely enough, and were now out of contact. Except for Wilson and his boys, Jimmy was on his own.

As Jimmy's adrenaline rose in the darkness of the woods, the cover officers remained stationary. Were they gripped by fear? Each one waiting for someone else to act? To them there were only one or possibly two suspects. They'd seen only Wilson get in the car with Jimmy. Neither Jimmy's return trip to the El Tavern Motel, where Wilson was seen waving his hand to someone, nor one of the surveillance officer's sightings of the three teenage accomplices walking toward the river, triggered any suspicion of a gang operation. The surveillance team members continued to lay back so that the dealer would not "get hinky." They laid so far back that they could neither hear nor see Jimmy. They might as well have been covering him from the top of a mountain in the distant Sierras.

Wilson continued toward the river, stopped and fished down in the pipework to pull up a parcel of white powder. No one made a move. Wilson showed his package to Jimmy, who simply turned to walk back to the 280ZX. For the second time, he came within little more than an arm's length from Lani.

From his blind, Lani thought Jimmy was looking straight at him as the officer walked through the brush, back to the safety of his car. It was at that instant that Wilson took control, effectively forcing the collective hand of his team of teenage desperados. He could not allow Jimmy to get back to the street where he would discover the real value of the package for which he was to hand over the $16K.

It was while Jimmy unwittingly faced the youngest of the gang of four that Wilson decided to act. When teenage Lani hesitated in his blind despite the target being in knife range, Wilson went hands on. He got an arm around Jimmy's neck and told his mates to attack.

"I'm going to kill you, motherfucker," exclaimed a surprised and enraged Jimmy.

"He's got a gun!" exclaimed Wilson.

For a long moment, all three of the boys froze, each waiting for one of the others to act, as Jimmy fought furiously to break away. Lani went first. He charged the short distance to Jimmy, who had his back to him, and plunged his long fixed-blade into the officer's back. Lani's butcher knife entered what he called Jimmy's left love handle from the back, perhaps inflicting only a superficial wound. It would take forensic evidence to later paint a clear picture.

When Lani stabbed Jimmy, the officer spun around and grabbed the boy's knife hand. It was a move taught in the Weaponless Defense classes in all police academies and the military, and a tactic that a cop prays he will never need since few expect the technique to be successful. It worked for Jimmy. As he snared Lani by the hand and threatened to kill him, he twisted the knife away from his own belly.

The knife fell. Lani broke Jimmy's grasp and bolted. Again, he heard Jimmy roar in pain and repeat, "I'm going to kill you."

As Lani ran, Wilson wrestled with Jimmy, urging his remaining fellows to join the fray. The officer fought back with his hands and fists, popping Wilson in the head during the struggle. It was turning into a fair fight since the remaining two members of Wilson's team continued to hesitate.

Wilson grappled with Jimmy, who tried to wrestle free or perhaps even pin Wilson. "Stab him, stab him," Wilson screamed at his backup. He was doing all he could to restrain Jimmy, who, by then, knew it was life or death.

Jimmy yelled loud enough to alert anyone within earshot, but his words died in the woods.

Wilson fought harder, encouraging his backups while hanging onto Jimmy's neck.

Lani didn't see that. He was running hard to the east, on Idlewild Drive toward the Keystone Bridge several hundred yards away, which would take him back across the river. He didn't stop or come back. He had been the first to attack, but Jimmy's defensive reaction overwhelmed him instantly. He ran hard, fueled by adrenalin and fear. He was not feeling tough. He realized that he had buried a knife in a fellow human being. He didn't know that he had attacked a cop, but he did know that the close combat he experienced was not the thrill he expected.

As Lani fled, 18-year-old Stites joined the fight. Unlike Lani, Stites did not strike once and run. He lunged at Jimmy repeatedly with his butcher knife. Wilson only had to hold on. One thrust entered Jimmy's chest to the right of center and penetrated several inches into the right lung. The path of the blade was down and to the left. Another deep thrust sent the stainless steel into Jimmy's chest a few inches below the armpit and penetrated downward and to the right.

The long blade plunged into Jimmy's core, inflicting deep wounds. Stites would state later that it was Olausen who furiously stabbed Jimmy and that he, Stites, only stabbed Jimmy after Wilson commanded him to and then ran away. But knives leave tracks of their own and examination of the wounds later would produce an accurate tale of the seconds-long, bloody and sweaty conflict.

Jimmy slowed and sagged to the ground, probably within less than two minutes after being stabbed by Lani.

"Don't...do it again," the fallen officer pleaded. "Don't –." He dropped to his knees, gasping, coughing blood, his consciousness fading.

The boys together stabbed Jimmy at least five times, each time feeling the blade penetrate smoothly into his body. Jimmy stopped fighting and the boys stopped stabbing. Stites, unharmed but finally unnerved, followed Lani's example and raced from the rocky riverbank through the bushes and between the trees, barely able to discern a path in the shades of black and not so black. As he went, he hurled his butcher knife into the silvery waters of the Truckee, a hopeless attempt at ablution. Having eased the pressure on his psyche, he stopped and listened, feeling mixed emotions of accomplishment and trepidation. He heard only water gurgling over and around the darkly brooding boulders and lapping at the river's banks. He began walking toward the El Tavern Motel, where he expected to find his roommate, Lani. As he fled, Wilson and Olausen stood by watching Jimmy, who was fading fast.

All of this—the ambush, the grunts and shouts of the attack and struggle, the flight of Lani and later Stites—was either ignored or missed by the surveillance team. The men all stayed back and they ignored whatever "wire" contact they had. That chafed the nerves of at least one of Jimmy's cover officers. He wanted to move in at the time Jimmy was being knifed. What, if anything, he heard or saw has yet to be told. He told the others, "There are transmission problems; we gotta go in, you know, it's not right."

Sergeant Brown, a man whose stomach was the only thing bigger than his ego, refused.

Right about that time, Jimmy quickly began losing control. As the last thrust was inflicted, Jimmy reached the point where fight was replaced by fear. No longer in the rage of combat, he begged to be allowed to live. His cover officers either did not hear or ignored his entreaties.

While the undercover cop was on his knees, Wilson ordered his accomplice to cut Jimmy's throat. Olausen halfheartedly complied, but merely succeeded at lacerating Jimmy's chin with the sharpened edge of the folding knife. He discovered, if in fact he was trying to finish Jimmy, that it was shockingly difficult to slice through a human throat to a sufficient depth to cut the carotid artery and ensure rapid death.

Olausen later denied the attempted *coup de grace*. He said that when he was trying to flee, holding his Buck knife in his hand, he cut someone he later concluded was Jimmy.

"I'm crawling up the slope (the bank just south of the pump house), and somebody grabs me by the shoulders and I don't know who it is," Olausen said, long after the killing. "He pushes me down and I punch. I know I made contact because I hit bone and teeth. The punch knocked the knife out of my hand."

Regardless of the actual circumstances, Olausen lost any belief about being a tough guy. He and Wilson stood by as Jimmy pitched forward, uttering that the money was in the car. The words are believed to be his last.

"Just lay down," Olausen said. "We won't hurt you anymore. It's over."

He moaned and blood gurgled in his throat.

Olausen and Wilson decided then that Jimmy was dead. Even after Jimmy had been stabbed, the narcotics section allowed a puzzling course of events that yet awaits explanation to take place.

Jimmy had sixteen thousand dollars in "buy money" in a cloth bag marked *Stash* in his car. After deciding he was dead, Wilson and Olausen lifted Jimmy from the ground and, with his legs dragging, carried him to the 280ZX and loaded him through the hatchback. As the dome light of the open hatch illuminated the blanched features of Jimmy Hoff, they unceremoniously hoisted him up and dumped him into the back of the car, where small amounts of blood and dirt soiled the immaculate interior of the car his fiancée had loaned him.

"Getting enough exercise?" one of the newly-bloodied youngsters asked his partner.

According to the cops, that bit of dark levity was heard over the body wire that Jimmy had left in the car.

Despite the strange occurrence in and around the car, the cops staggered about undecided, afraid or unwilling to act. Unlike them, Wilson and Olausen suffered no such indecision. They took control, looking forward to the rush of possessing sixteen thousand in crisp, green American hundreds. The idea of a large amount of money was quickly making the queasiness of stabbing a fellow human fade away. It was quite a score for the two idlers who had never done more than look at such sums of money in the casinos.

Bravado setting in, Wilson and Olausen got into the 280ZX and headed onto Idlewild Drive. Before fleeing the murder scene, they searched the car and found the bag of money. They also located two guns, one in the shopping bag and one in the glove compartment, but left the firearms where they found them.

It was 1:44 a.m. when the car emerged from its hidden parking place. Wilson, nervous as well as exhilarated, accelerated rapidly on Idlewild Drive and headed toward the El Tavern Motel. He didn't know it, but one of the surveillance officers was driving via a slightly different route to the motel. At 1:55, he saw the 280ZX drive west on Fourth. That was a couple of minutes after he'd seen it on Vine Street, a north-south alternate to Keystone. Vine parallels the larger street and runs north from the river across several streets including Fourth.

In minutes the 280ZX pulled up to the motel and Wilson and Olausen went into the room shared by Lani and Stites. The four killers came up with a plan and cleared the room. As they did, they helped themselves to a sheet which they later claimed—against conflicting evidence—was the same slit-damaged one that had been on the mattress when

Lani and Stites purportedly used it to practice knife thrusts. The boys also bagged up their clothing and effects in preparation to leave in the early morning darkness.

Although the boys parked the 280ZX where the surveillance team couldn't observe the entire vehicle or the movement of the suspects, the car was spotted just ten minutes after it had been parked.

Inside the car, Jimmy's body, which filled the back of the two-seater, was curled up in the luggage compartment, beneath the glass hatch. The boys covered their grisly cargo with the purloined sheet. Wilson was behind the wheel while Lani sat on Olausen's lap in the passenger seat. It would later be alleged that at that point Jimmy Hoff was still alive.

Chapter 2

THE CALL OUT

It was Monday morning. Ray Vega's day off. He worked swing shift, 4 p.m. to midnight. Sunday, June 24 was the usual, a warm day following a cool night. He had worked that Sunday and was looking forward to a family day this Monday the 25th. His expectation was not to be borne out. This would not be a quiet day with the kids. Typically, Reno was quiet on Mondays. The tourists got up late on Sunday, ate a bucketful of creampuffs, bacon and donuts at one of the casino buffets and headed back over the Sierras to their California homes. It was the time before the Indian casinos all but killed Reno. The large gambling corporations were still reaping huge profits in 1979 and downtown Reno was cooking. Downtown was Ray's beat, but not this day.

Ray was new to Reno but had spent eight years working the street in California. Now he was a street cop in Nevada, wearing a blue suit with a cheesy gold stripe running down the outside of each leg. One of the other big city refugees called it a bellhop uniform with a gold star. Reno PD was a strange place to Ray—a lot of crime, some of it coming from the other cops, including the top brass. The rest of the crime came from the transient population that came for the casinos and whorehouses. It was said that every serious crook in America would at some time visit Reno. Despite the high level of crime, RPD was surprisingly backward. A lot of the troops were still living in the past century. In the poorer, darker part of town, it was referred to as the "Mississippi of the West." It was all new to Ray, a big city cop in backasswards Reno.

Around lunchtime on Monday, Ray got a call from Officer Holly. He knew her well enough to be on a first name basis and had worked the street with her. She called from the station and her strained tone made it clear that it was not a personal call. She said she was assigned to call everyone who was off duty and inform them that a cop was missing. Veteran officer Jimmy Hoff had disappeared during a drug transaction and they, the cops, did not know where he was. They just knew he was gone. Ray did not hesitate. He asked, "Can I come in to work and look for him?" She hesitated after the quick response, and then said, "Yeah, I think that's okay." She told him that Jimmy "went missing around midnight and that there were suspects." Her voice came across the land wire with an urgency that quickened his pulse and started the bile to rise in his throat.

This was not his first rodeo. In his first eight months on the street in a large urban department, three uniformed brothers were shot down. The first was killed on Ray's first day out of the academy in the district he was assigned to. The realization that a fellow officer had been murdered on the street where he worked every day caused his hands to tremble slightly. The victim officer was shot in the chest with a .38 by a whacked-out psycho. Two more cops were shot and murdered in separate incidents in the following eight months. He had worked with one of the three murder victims and had ties to the other two based on assignment and shift. So, an officer as a murder victim was not new to Ray Vega.

When he heard that Jimmy Hoff was missing, Ray's first thought was that he must be dead. He had seen others pay the price for taking foolish risks. Just as quickly, he told himself that it didn't matter, Jimmy might be alive. Ray's wife and kids were there in the house when the call came. He headed for the bedroom where his uniform hung in the closet. As he quickly dressed, he told his pregnant wife that he was going to work. "One of the narcs is missing." She didn't say much or argue. She could tell by his edgy tone that he was in a "Don't fuck with me" mood. He didn't tell her that it sounded like the narc was already dead. He had deduced, based on the amount of time that had elapsed, that Jimmy Hoff was already gone. But you never know and besides, he's alive until you look into his "fixed and dilated" eyes.

Ray was known as a *boomer* at Reno PD. That was a term used for guys who came to Reno after holding cop jobs in other parts. Despite his experience, he had no "juice." Reno PD was famous for its anti-outsider attitude. On his way to the police station he told himself not to expect a good assignment. As the new guy, he was not hopeful about getting assigned somewhere he might have a real chance at catching the shitbags who did something to a brother officer. Nevertheless, he was off to do what he could, even if it was to direct traffic.

Even though he only had scant contact with Jimmy, Ray liked and respected him as both a cop and a good guy. Jimmy had what all good narcs needed: a likable personality and guts. He had been in the army for six years and maintained the erect bearing schooled into him by the drill sergeants. As a soldier, he had marched with the Army honor guard, a special detail of guys who carried the flag and marched at ceremonies. Certainly, his boyish good looks, tractability and attention to detail made him a likely candidate for that honor. His military posture could have detracted from his role as a narcotics user had he not been so friendly and personable. In addition to those qualities, you could tell that he just plain wanted to be a good cop and most importantly, he loved catching crooks. Ray figured that was why Jimmy was not a sergeant yet; he was too busy hooking and booking bad guys.

Ray had one encounter with Jimmy prior to June 25. He had arrested some kid for possession of dope and was leaving the jail when he ran into Jimmy and another narc. Ray had worked undercover in a big city and knew the business. But he knew better than to appear to be a know-it-all. He went easy.

Addressing both the narcs, he offered: "Hey if you guys are interested I just booked a kid for dope. He seemed willing to talk, if you guys want to talk to him."

The narc with Jimmy retorted loudly, "We don't have time for some bullshit with that fuck."

Ray responded: "Hey, you never know, he might be a pisspot but you never know…"

"We ain't fuckin' around with no pisspot when we've got real work to do" the narc replied, interrupting Ray in mid-sentence.

"Okay man, okay," Ray said as he turned his back to the bigmouth and walked away. He had quickly learned that Hoff's partner had, as they said in the big city, an alligator mouth and a hummingbird ass.

While the bigmouth talked shit, Jimmy Hoff said nothing but turned his gaze away from Ray.

Later, Ray told one of the other veteran cops that he should have "bitch slapped" the bigmouthed "punk," but he was on probation and might have lost his job over it.

Ray ran into Jimmy later that day and spoke with him for the first time. Jimmy Hoff held out his hand and introduced himself with a firm handshake.

"Hey, thanks for the tip on that kid you booked earlier. We'll check it out, who knows?"

Ray said, "Yeah, who knows? "

"We'll go upstairs and interview him. I appreciate all the help we can get from patrol. You know we're all on the same team."

Jimmy did not mention the bigmouth narc but was clearly apologizing for the other cop's rudeness. Ray didn't say much but filed Jimmy Hoff's name under "stand-up guy." It wasn't just the apology that formed a lasting impression, it was the way he leaned in and made eye-contact when he spoke. He meant what he said.

After the discussion regarding the possible informant, Ray had only passing contact with Jimmy. He did learn a bit about him, since the other cops liked to talk about their popular officer "Jimmy the narc." Jimmy was an athlete and played for the Reno PD basketball team in the Police Olympics every year. He was apparently a bit of a star. Ray was not surprised that Jimmy excelled at a team sport. He was the epitome of the jock who was voted the team captain. He had it all, including the "popularity gene" according to one of the salty older cops. He also found out that Jimmy was popular with the ladies, as might be expected of a guy described by a female clerk as "male model good looking."

It was early afternoon when Ray reached the Police station. He had a day's growth of beard as he walked into the Watch Commander's office. He skipped the small talk and asked where the lieutenant wanted him.

"Just get your radio and go to Keystone and Fourth. That's where two of the suspects were last seen," the lieutenant told him. "Check in with the command post. They'll let you know where you're needed."

"Got it. What do we know about the suspects?"

The lieutenant described Wilson and Olausen as "two white males, young, maybe twenty, six foot, slim."

"Are they armed?" Ray asked.

"Don't know, but Hoff has been missing since about 1 a.m."

Ray just grunted.

"They found Hoff's car in that neighborhood and one of the suspects dropped a knife. There was blood in the car." The lieutenant continued. He explained that the narcs had pursued Jimmy's car into Dog Valley, about ten miles west of Reno, and that two searches were going on: one for Jimmy, who might have been left in Dog Valley, and another for two suspects who ran from one of the uniformed cops.

Ray was one of the many officers who had not even known of the narcotics operation but had now been called out to search for the fugitives. To a person, they all knew Jimmy Hoff and liked him. Uniforms who'd worked midnight shift stayed on into the day. Other officers on their days off heard reports of the search and volunteered to join in. Each searcher was assigned to either the area of the abandoned car or to the area where they knew the car had gone, Dog Valley.

Chief of Police Jim Parker arrived at the station before dawn and commanded the troops be split between the Dog Valley search and the one for "two white males" already identified as Wilson and Olausen. There was little discussion about Jimmy's fate among the searchers. Someone with medical training opined that there was little if any time left to find Jimmy alive. Despite the lousy odds, many remained optimistic.

Parker had about one hundred officers searching, gathering evidence and knocking on doors. They were both on-duty and off-duty and represented the RPD, the Washoe County Sheriff's Department and other local agencies. Many scoured the area where Wilson and Olausen were last seen fleeing on foot. The search he initiated in the Dog Valley area was out of the city and partially in California. The Sheriff's office in California was not notified until much later.

The question that ran through the mind of Ray Vega was what to do if and when the suspects were found. The idea of coming upon the killers out of the city, where there were no witnesses, surely invited fantasies of an "officer involved shooting." A couple of rounds placed center mass and two dead crooks. It could never be questioned with only one surviving witness: the shooter. But then, how would any information be gathered? At least one of the fugitives would have to survive so that intelligence could be obtained and Jimmy Hoff could be located. There was no easy and clean answer. Anyone who was found would have to survive long enough to talk and this would preclude killing them both. One of them would have to be captured without significant harm coming to him, at least until all the suspects were identified and Jimmy Hoff was accounted for.

As the day wore on and Jimmy Hoff was not found and the four suspects were not in custody, the manhunt heated up. The searchers had descriptions of Wilson and Olausen and they had a good idea that those two were still on foot in the same area.

Ray later remarked, "Olausen and Wilson were not exactly rocket scientists." They hadn't fled far and they hadn't concealed themselves well. They had no weapons and the cops were armed and ready to use deadly force. More cops were coming to work on their own time, working overtime. The city and its environs were under search by officers whose emotions ranged from nearly professional detachment to fervent anger. It was the type of anger engendered by the presumed murder of one's brother.

Meanwhile, Wilson and Olausen did the only thing they could do at that time: they stayed hidden and slept into the afternoon in the quiet brush.

While they slept, Bruce Richard Gates, an agent in the Nevada Division of Investigation or NDI, a subdivision of the State's Department of

Transportation and Public Safety, drew an assignment on the 25th of June to help Reno police in their search for Jimmy and the crooks. The agency assists rural county agencies: investigates state employee misdeeds and conducts narcotics investigations. The narcotics function gets the most attention and NDI's narcotics officers work with law enforcement agencies across the state and are part of several Combined Narcotics Task Forces. Gates knew Jimmy and the other narcs.

Gates' assignment that day was beating the brush down by the river. Ray Vega was also out in the brush about 200 yards to the east. The search was conducted willy-nilly with no organized pattern and Ray was hoping no one got excited and shot blindly into the brush. It was like opening day of deer season to the power of ten. In the early afternoon, Gates and a partner, John Drew, searched the trailer courts next to the El Tavern Motel where Olausen and Wilson had been staying and soon the two investigators were in the brushy areas between Fourth Street and Interstate 80. They checked the trailer parks, spaces between and behind the rows of trailer houses and the surrounding brushy areas. Gates was to recall that, "We crisscrossed that area behind there."

Gates and his partner discovered some fresh footprints and followed them, and then they "saw what looked like clothing in the bushes." The "clothing" moved. The two NDI officers climbed over a fence and crept closer. They were about two hundred yards west of where the 280ZX had been abandoned. Their find: "Two subjects laying in the bushes and they appeared to be sleeping." They drew their guns, "proned out" the two boys and demanded identification. They got it—Wilson and Olausen.

"Immediately we advised them of their rights and then we got the handcuffs on them," Gates explained later. "There was a blue vest lying on the ground when I pulled them out of the bushes and I picked that up."

What did he do next?

"I could see some money in one of the pockets. I didn't go any further from there. I just held onto the vest until Officer Jerry Hazen arrived at the scene approximately seven minutes later and I turned the vest over to him."

He said the bills he saw "looked like hundreds" but he couldn't swear to it. In his recitation, Gerald Hazen of the Reno Police Department's Detective Division described meeting Gates and Drew.

"We found them on the other side of the six-foot fence in the trailer park next to the irrigation ditch, two suspects sitting against the fence handcuffed, at which time we assisted the two suspects over the top of the fence and Officer Gates handed me the blue down vest."

One of the soon-to-be defendants later described the "assist" over the fence as being launched head first over the fence by an angry Reno cop. Not exactly the outcome the boys had imagined when they concocted their plan. From start to finish, the drug bust had gone so horribly wrong it defied just about everyone's expectations, even in a place with as much drug-related experience as Reno.

Chapter 3

BUYING DOPE

Northwestern Nevada, frigid in winter, arid in summer and windy all the time, has always been a hard place to make a living. Gold and silver helped a century ago. Then speedy divorces became a large revenue producer. Legal prostitution and gambling were always there. With them came patrons and workers who drank hard, smoked and earned a living separating the gullible from their gelt. The infiltration of drugs was inevitable.

The soldiers in the sometimes-half-hearted war against drugs are the police, be they street cops or members of narcotics squads, the feds or the combined narcotics task forces. Not surprisingly, many of the cops in the anti-drug campaign are cowboys. They are in it for the hunt, the excitement, and only after the adrenalin wears off do they consider the ultimate aim. All good narcotics agents want to eradicate drugs, but the really good ones have fun doing it.

Like other departments across the nation, if not around the world, the Reno Police Department had committed its officers to drying up the river of drugs that virtually every day killed somebody's kid. Everybody knew the obvious, that is, that every sale could not be stopped, that every illicit importation could not be interdicted. What could be done was that dealers could be identified and jailed or discouraged in other ways. That took them off the street and made those who would replace them hesitate. Perfect, no, but helpful, yes.

The 1979 lore of the underworld was that gambling and drugs often went together. However, while gambling was legal, drugs were frowned upon. Reno had both a moral and a self-seeking interest in wiping out drugs. What was spent on the streets and in alleys couldn't be pissed away at the tables. So, Ricky Brown's squad had a job to do, and Jimmy Hoff had proven he was the ace on Brown's team.

A good investigator relies on all sources for his information. In the nether world of street drugs, the best sources of information are the informants. Officially identified in the files as confidential informants or C.I.'s, these snitches or "rats," as they're known, usually come to the cops because they're in trouble, occasionally because they like cops, and sometimes for money. Often, it's a combination of all three.

In Reno one such person was Anne Marie, who was in trouble with the law, in that situation known as having "a beef." The local cops had found out about her soliciting in bars and casinos and developed an interest in her. A background check turned up an arrest warrant from California, and officers arrested her in an apartment she had on Lake Street. There they found enough marijuana for a felony complaint. Serious conversation followed and the officers, finding her compliant, took her to the narcotics detail to work off her arrest by informing—becoming a snitch.

The police had a lot of leverage with Anne Marie. The fugitive warrant had been issued because she'd split rather than face an accusation of stealing forty-five thousand dollars' worth of jewelry.

"That was just a misunderstanding," she said later. "I never stole anything."

She wasn't prosecuted, but the suspicion was that the jewelry had belonged to the deceased wife of an attorney who may have been one of her tricks. The warrant and arrest led to an extensive relationship with the Reno Police Department and her agreement to "duke" Jimmy in to some dope dealers who would sell to him.

Anne Marie, who worked the streets and liked to stay stoned, had scored marijuana from Tom Wilson. She'd also heard him brag about being able to put a drug transaction together, and she wanted to impress Jimmy Hoff, the amiable, fair-haired narc with the quick smile. The ingredients were coming together.

C.I. Anne Marie started slowly but came to be a regular around RPD. She bragged about driving around in a pig load with Sergeant "Downtown" Brown. "He would cruise around town in this unmarked Ford that everyone could tell was a cop car. I think it had been a black and white that was repainted. Anyway, he'd be drinking beer and tossing 'dead Buds' out the window. I guess the regular cops didn't mess with him."

Anne Marie described Jimmy in glowing terms. He was a straight arrow. Despite her predilection for killer weed, she praised Jimmy for staying clean. "He didn't smoke dope and didn't hang out with anyone who did." She did whatever she could to assist her new friends at Reno PD. She was the go-to girl.

Generally, a narcotics transaction is set up in stages and progresses according to a general plan. First, there is a "duke in" or getting-to-know-you meeting where a small transaction is conducted.

Sometimes the first buy involves only the targeted seller and the snitch because a careful dope dealer does not welcome the risk of exposure to a stranger. In the classic case, the second or third transaction involves a larger buy, depending on the police agency's willingness to let the money "walk."

After several buys have been made, the narcs set the seller up with a large purchase for an irresistible amount of "flash money."

That final buy is the "buy/bust." There, ideally, extreme care is taken to control the players and minimize risk to officers and informants. Working with cowboys, of course, complicates control. Another reason for control is the collection of evidence in a way that will withstand the attacks of silk-suited defense lawyers sniffing at the money trail and often screaming entrapment.

Sometimes the buy will go down in the crook's pad, and a search warrant will have been prepared to serve simultaneously with the arrest. A buy/bust inside the seller's abode is never entirely safe because the cop is on the dealer's turf, but at least a crook will seldom plan a rip-off inside his own place. The obvious reason is that the victim, be he a burn target or cop, will know where to return to square things up with the rip-off artist. Besides, there are often women and children in the house.

The safest buy will go down in a motel or hotel room chosen by the narcs. This provides a semi-public forum for the deal and it operates to avoid violence. Setting up a buy/bust in a rented room gives the agency the chance to get equipment in place in advance to record the operation. Moreover, an adjacent room with a common door to the transaction room or at least a convenient hallway helps in case the operation goes sour and quick intervention is needed. Often, however, drug deals go down on the street, in parking lots, in parks or in such public places as casinos and ordinarily quiet bars. In these situations, backup teams turn to close surveillance, body wires and car microphones that transmit by way of hidden mikes to reduce risk to their undercover cop or C.I.

For an operation to succeed, no matter where it goes down, there must be sufficient manpower. In the days before Jimmy met Tom Wilson, the narcs often worked closely with Vice in the RPD. When backup was needed, the narcs would call on Vice to get necessary support.

While Jimmy served as a narc, Sergeant Charles (Chuck) Reavis oversaw Vice. Like Sergeant Brown, Chuck was well liked and was affectionately known as Blinky because of his tendency to flutter his eyelids when speaking.

Unlike Brown, Blinky did not intimidate others with his physical presence. He was blond and good-looking with skinny, boyish arms and a neck to match. He had a likeable, non-threatening presence, especially with the ladies. He also was known for his ability to drink a lot and a predilection to marry often.

"Vice" can mean many things in the worlds of immorality and depravity, but in Reno in 1979 it meant prostitution. The Vice Squad specialized in keeping tabs on the ordinary as well as the extraordinary *filles de joie* in town, including the independents who worked casinos.

It must have made sense to someone in RPD administration to put handsome and hard-drinking Reavis in charge since the Vice detail ordinarily had to work casino bars. Vice officers seemed very willing to sacrifice their livers to control the battalions of naughties who subtly displayed their frowned-upon promises of pleasure on the street or in the plushy, carefully lit and carefully unlit palaces where every spin can be a win.

Blinky had worked as a California highway patrolman before he drifted over the Sierras in the Seventies to join the RPD. He found a friend in Brown and became one of his drinking buddies.

Vice Officers Jim Atyeo and Fred Bradley, older troops with significant backgrounds and experience in police work, joined Reavis to assist the narcs. Atyeo had a long career as a non-commissioned officer in the Marine Corp before he became a Reno cop.

Atyeo wasn't big, but he was Marine lean with a ready toughness and outspoken attitude. Although he held the rank of patrolman he rarely hesitated to advise others and readily dressed down anyone he thought wasn't pulling his weight. This was especially true if it looked like he would have to do any more work than was absolutely necessary. He was in his forties and perfect for Vice because he didn't fit the cop stereotype. He looked like a middle-aged guy out to have a drink and some fun, the guy the working girls looked for. Neither did Detective Fred Bradley, one of the oldest cops still working the street. Bradley was like Jimmy with twenty extra years. Even when he took you to jail, you had to like him.

Lieutenant Larry Dennison supervised both Narcotics and Vice but was curiously absent both from the record and the scene of the buy/bust. He was a young supervisor who, like Eubanks, started as a cadet and grew up in police work. Ray, in his usual sarcastic tone said: "they were both halfwits who never held down a real job."

Dennison and Reavis got along well. Such was hardly the case with Ricky Brown. He wasted no time intimidating Dennison, thereby making the lieutenant happy to allow Sergeant Brown to run his small unit with very little interference. That was the way Brown liked to operate and the way he did operate. He would continue in that manner in the Jimmy Hoff fiasco, and he would lead his own troops plus Reavis, Atyeo and Detective Fred Bradley with neither interference nor direct involvement from the lieutenant.

On June 24, 1979, all the cops from the Vice and Narcotics details were depending on Anne Marie to put this deal together. She was more than just a snitch by then. She considered herself a friend to the narcs who used her as bait in a deadly expedition.

Chapter 4

GOING WRONG, THE PLANNING

Anne Marie lolled on her bed, her white cotton blouse pulling loose from the waist of her plaid skirt. It wasn't a mini, but its hem had hitched up past mid-thigh. She had shucked her loafers and they lay at angles on the floor. She pursed her lips on the smoked-down doobie and sucked hard, then waved it away with a flourish, holding her breath. A quarter of a minute passed.

"Oh, Steve-O," she said, forcing a whisper, "you can look, but you better not touch. That's for paying customers."

"Shee-it, tell me." Olausen reached for her hand, took the doobie and settled back on the thinly upholstered chair. He grinned at her, his blue eyes twinkling, then took a hit, rolling his head back and holding his breath.

It was easy being with her. She was tall and long-legged, and he didn't mind if she held out and used it on the streets to make a living. Sure as hell, what she earned as a waitress at the Riverside wouldn't keep her. Everybody had to do something, and it was okay—hell, the coolest—that she let him hang out in her room and smoke to while away the early part of the night. She wasn't too ambitious though. Work a little, buy a baggie or two from Wilson, smoke a little, work a little. But he didn't care. She was fun to be with.

"My turn," she said, waving to tell him to return the nearly spent doobie.

"Yo." He chuckled to himself when she bent toward him and her horn-rimmed glasses slipped down her nose and came to rest crookedly across her face. It made her look cute, like a schoolgirl, only cuter. She was perfect, working the lounges and looking like a college kid. She was cool. He watched her brush her long straight hair back before reclining to inhale again.

"You are one fun lady," he said, eyeing her under half-closed lids.

"My wild phase," she cooed. "Not forever, but for now. For a while."

"You got it," he said, never entertaining any idea the pretty blonde was working as a snitch for the local narcs. She gave not a hint that she wanted to please the star narc, Jimmy Hoff. Anne Marie's Lake Street digs provided her with a venue to set up drug deals. One of her neighbors had been a pimp who sold heroin. She set him up by bringing in Jimmy's fellow narc, John Douglas, a black officer and an Air Guardsman, who had a razor sharp tongue. That made her something of a pet in the Narcotics Unit. She started hanging out with the narcs, having a few drinks, developing amiable relationships, doing ride-alongs and developing a professional relationship with Jimmy. She quickly worked off her beef, but she kept up C.I. work because she wanted to. "I wanted to help the cops," she said. "It made me feel good."

After ratting out the pimp/heroin dealer, Anne Marie decided that it was a good time to move. She found a place at the Reef Hotel where Olausen and Wilson were working as handymen in return for a room. She was only slightly older than they were, but she was a good deal more street-smart. It was her job to make the connection for Jimmy, who then would come in as the heavy to make the buys. Wilson and Olausen soon became her hottest prospects. She'd heard Wilson brag that he could put a deal together and he'd sold her some weed. She'd make good use of him.

Wilson was young and virile. Only the softness of his jawline kept him from looking like a Greek god. His dark hair hung a little past his collar framing a strong face with a bulbous forehead. He was good looking, but his deep-set brooding eyes bothered Anne Marie. So did his compulsion to pass for twenty-one and play at casino tables—a gambler, not a worker who always "looked for the hustle."

Anne Marie had little esteem for Wilson who tried to be as charming as Olausen. He was reasonably pleasant and easy to be with when he dropped a little pot off in her room. That, however, was hardly a sufficient reason not to hand him over to the narcs. She was ready to please Jimmy.

"Love that dude," she mumbled to Olausen through sweet smelling smoke. "Those eyes—"

"I thought you said he was really mean, like bad. Like he beats you."

"Oh no, not me. I'm his favorite." She propped herself up on her pillow to stare meaningfully at Olausen. "They say that, but I just look at those eyes. It's all okay."

Olausen sighed. Maybe women did like to be kicked around. Hard to understand. Hard to understand her friends too, unless it was the money.

Anne Marie introduced one of those friends, an old drunk named Bud, to Olausen and Wilson. Bud hung out at the Reef, and the two youngsters had seen him in the bar while they were working. He claimed to have served a stretch in prison, bragged about it like it made him tough. The boys were young and sufficiently impressed. Bud, however, wasn't tough, just old and drunk. Olausen had an aversion to the old man and spoke little with him. That wasn't true of Wilson.

Bud seemed ancient and wise since he'd been to prison. He engaged Wilson in small talk. Having an audience and the prospect of making a dollar or two, he wasted little time dredging up the subject of selling dope. He said the buyers were out there, waiting to spend. Like Anne Marie, he was hustling.

The drugs and high life soon got to Olausen and Wilson. Unreliable, they were fired as kitchen workers at the Sahara and then they got kicked out of the Reef. After that, they'd been relegated to crashing with friends. Among those friends were Fred Stites and David Lani who let them sleep in their room at the El Tavern Motel on West Fourth.

They could visit Anne Marie and Bud, but those two were hardly the type to give them money. The boys found themselves needing cash in a gambler's hell hole where money always flows the wrong way. A brisk pawn shop trade testifies to that, but they had nothing to pawn.

As Wilson alternately bragged and aired his problems as a new member of the homeless population, Anne Marie paid close attention. He needed to generate some cash, he said. Having no house and no money didn't cut it. That was when she clued him in about Jimmy the "bad-assed" pimp who had money. That was on or about June 22, 1979, a Friday.

Jimmy, she said, qualified as a real heavy. He was a pimp, a dope dealer and "no one to fuck with." She portrayed him as a notoriously bad hombre and the type who motivated his working girls with severe beatings. He was well-heeled, and in fact, she said, it just happened he'd mentioned he was trying to cop large quantities of coke. Wilson's antennae went up.

Bud, the old-timer, offered a few meaningless words of advice to look important. Anne Marie smiled a little, and went on. It was working. She allowed as how she was willing to put Wilson in touch with the right people, Jimmy among them, and all she asked for was some of the action, a cash payoff.

Wilson's eyes stayed on her as he asked questions. He started scheming while she talked. Suppose, he thought, we set up a coke sale to this Jimmy the pimp, this hustler with a nice car.

Wilson was mentally savoring the profit to be made on the deal. After all, hadn't Anne Marie, the knowledgeable one, said Jimmy had the cash and would pay a good price? The girl seemed to be acting in good faith, and even better, she didn't seem to realize that Wilson could be a scam artist. It was a scam on a scam—she too had a secret agenda. Jimmy was scamming Wilson through Anne Marie and she was scamming both. Everyone was scamming everyone.

As Wilson shaped and reshaped his easy-money scheme, a discontented Olausen yearned to go back home. On the same Friday that Wilson was talking about "the deal," Olausen, out of joy and aced out of his romance with the singer from the Gilded Cage, called his dad to ask about returning home. No, his dad said. He did not want to stress his new relationship. Olausen felt he was on the road to nowhere. Still, Reno was closing in. He headed for the Greyhound Bus Station on First Street about mid-morning—just about broke and thinking of Southern California.

"I'm ready to go, I'm on foot going toward the bus station and jaywalking, and Tom pulls up in her (the singer's) white Camaro. I said I was going to L.A."

Wilson had stopped in the middle of the block in the Camaro. As traffic backed up behind him, he leaned on Olausen to stay with him. Olausen resisted and walked on. He was in the bus station when Wilson confronted him again.

"I'll get my stuff," Wilson said. "I'll go pick up my stuff…I'll leave with you." Olausen listened to the only person who seemed to want him around. He faltered and returned to Stites and Lani's room in the El Tavern. Wilson produced a bottle of Everclear and "lots of pot, probably about a quarter pound of it," Olausen remembered. He proceeded to dull his melancholy with smoke and drink while Wilson left to, as he put it, "clear up a couple of problems."

Olausen recalled that when Wilson returned, he didn't have his belongings or indicate he was ready to travel. Instead, he told Olausen, "Hey, I got to check this guy out." He was referring to Jimmy and formulating his plan. The "checking" was apparently through Anne Marie, now part of his gang.

The destitution shared by Wilson and Olausen hardly cast them as heavy duty dope dealers, but that wasn't Anne Marie's concern. For her, it would please her newfound friends in the Narcotics Unit. She was fixed on turning a different trick for Jimmy. She was bent on delivering two chumps to him. In one version of the story, she vilified him as a pimp, knowing and appreciating that he was an undercover RPD narcotics investigator. In another, it appeared she was just bragging about knowing a big shot with money.

As Anne Marie carried on the charade, Wilson went so far as to say he had been around dope for some time and that he had the "connects" in Sacramento to put a substantial deal down. In fact, he told Anne Marie that a friend was offering ten ounces for sixteen thousand. Wilson told Anne Marie that he wanted to sell his entire package all at once—no small deals—and asked her who she knew that might be interested. Wilson wanted to put the deal down in one fell swoop, all the dope for all the cash.

Olausen played the background guy. He nearly always accompanied Wilson but just stood back quietly, a spectator, not a participant. He was there as Wilson's friend. Olausen never talked to Anne Marie or Bud about the deal with Jimmy. He was the silent partner. Wilson was the real target.

Was it possible that Anne Marie believed Wilson could produce a large amount of dope to sell to the cops? Only she knows. She set the boys up for a big-league deal to ingratiate herself with the narcs. What she didn't and couldn't know was that she was setting Jimmy up to die.

Afterwards, on that Friday, she made a call to Jimmy, who said he'd like to be put in touch with Tom Wilson. Jimmy was ready to move, ready to make the buy that night. He quickly contacted Deputy District Attorney Bruce Laxalt, a young prosecutor. He had gotten to know the legendary narc by handling narcotics prosecutions in the D.A.'s office. "I thought he walked on water," Laxalt said. "He was dynamic and laid back at the same time...detached and there." Laxalt told Jimmy he too was ready.

There were two conversations between Wilson and Anne Marie that Friday: one in late afternoon and the second at night. It was after the first that she made her call. Then hours went by with no move on Wilson's part. Oddly, there was no attempt to test the reliability of either party or the quality of the product. Wilson told the confidential informant he would only deal with one person, and she couldn't be there when the deal went down. No one else either.

Tom Wilson hung back. He didn't contact Jimmy on Friday night, and he didn't contact him on Saturday. Jimmy, hungry to make the big buy, waited for the call. He even let that hunger interfere with his best friend and team member Randy Flocchini's wedding party.

Wilson was out to make money—more money than a simple commission. By doing a burn, he kept it all. Anne Marie was the duke in but denied being privy to the "burn" part of the conversation. In any event, she made the deal between Jimmy and Wilson happen.

Wilson approached her cold with the idea to sell ten ounces of cocaine for sixteen thousand dollars. Later, it was mentioned that they might do a burn on Jimmy and, according to the C.I., she was adamantly opposed. She also reported that she warned Jimmy about the possible burn.

To convince Wilson and his young mates that Jimmy was a for-real badass and not a cop, she reportedly told them that he was a woman-beating pimp who sold narcotics to school kids. Whether this was a figment of the polluted imaginations of the four boys or the product of Anne Marie's salesmanship is uncertain, but as the deal with the big guy (Jimmy) approached, Wilson and his mates convinced themselves that Jimmy was a truly rotten individual.

During the second Friday night conversation with Wilson, where Olausen stood silently by, Anne Marie gave Wilson "Jim's" phone number, in actuality the number to the phone in the narcotics detail. This single line into the Police Department was accessible only to the narcs who answered the phone as though it was a private line in someone's home. When Wilson rang the line, he believed that he was calling Jimmy at home.

Anne Marie had instructions to get Wilson to call. That night Wilson jotted down the number and said he'd call later. He did. He told Anne Marie the next day, Saturday, that he had talked to Jimmy on the phone and wanted to meet him—alone. Wilson stressed the alone part. He told her that, in his experience, cops would only deal with friends there. If Jimmy came without backup, he was not setting Wilson up. "Jim had to be alone." Anne Marie passed the condition on to Jimmy.

On Saturday night, Wilson told Anne Marie that he'd met Jim and they were working out a deal. He told her that she was going to get a cut of the money.

Hours later, about 1 a.m., Sunday, June 24, 1979, Wilson and Olausen showed up at Anne Marie's room and asked a new series of questions. They wanted to know all about him. She told them that his name was Jim Lucas and that he was a freelance photographer.

"Well," Wilson wanted to know, "are you and Jim Lucas good friends?"

"Sort of," she answered.

"If you want, we can really burn him good."

"No," she answered. "He is a friend of mine, I don't want to burn him. Nothing better happen to him."

Wilson had it wired. He was going to use baking soda as the bait, wrapped up to look like cocaine in small packages ready for sale. Baking soda and cocaine are vaguely similar but not enough to fool a sophisticated dope dealer. Soda is coarse, does not flake and has no color other than white. Still, it would require ingestion or a chemical test to tell the difference. Properly-trained narcotics officers do not do a taste test on suspected cocaine as depicted in the movies.

From the get-go, Wilson was rock steady. It took major balls, or major stupidity, for him to set up this burn. Anne Marie told him that Jim had lots of cash. He drove a nice car, dressed well and lived the high life. It was all a ruse, set up to trap those who let greed and self-indulgence rule their world. Wilson and Olausen thought that they would be living the high life—it would turn out to be the high road on the path to hell.

Once the deal got rolling, it moved fast. In about forty-eight hours, it went from negotiations with the snitch to a meet with Jimmy the pimp. The night train to hell was barreling down the tracks with Wilson at the throttle. Cannonball Tom did not have a hand on the brake. Olausen was enjoying the ride.

The plan was for Jimmy Hoff to arrive at a yet to be disclosed location with major cash in his pocket.

He was on the verge of making the largest hand-to-hand buy of powder (hard drugs) in the history of Reno. It was to be Jimmy's last buy, to go out on top. It was not meant to be his final act as a law enforcement officer. He was buying a large amount of cocaine. Wilson was running a crude game, the ultimate rip-off. But Jimmy was ready. No fear felt the young lion.

With the deal in the making, all the warning lights were going off but the cops were blind. When Jimmy and his backups had started the investigation involving Wilson and his teenage accomplices, it was already clear that the deal was wrong, it was tainted. Still, it went on. Anne Marie described Wilson and Olausen as hardly more than boys. Wilson had a record but was apparently never checked out. Had he been investigated, Jimmy would have known that he was dealing with a "burn artist." Even a casual glance would have told them Wilson did not appear to be someone who could produce any quantity of coke— one ounce, ten ounces, or even a gram. He was a youngster with no assets or acumen. He didn't even have a car, and he lived in a rat and roach motel on Fourth Street on someone else's dime.

Olausen was an 18-year-old bystander, hardly the heavy that could carry off this kind of a deal. There was never an indication that anybody in RPD checked him out either.

Wilson was to deliver ten ounces of ninety-seven percent pure cocaine, plus some "twenty-four-karat-gold" marijuana, the latter to be had for two hundred fifty a kilo. When the cops allowed themselves to believe that this was anything other than a burn, the first in a long and lethal string of blunders fell into place. The emperor was naked but no one would admit it.

There would be more unthinkable, impossible-to-undo blunders. Jimmy, even after having been warned of a burn, wanted to do the deal alone, blinded by the attraction of a sixteen thousand dollar buy.

Frank Torres talked to Jimmy the night before the deal went down. "He wanted me to go with him. We had Randy Flocchini's wedding party at the Hardy House. This was the 23rd or 24th, a Saturday night. He was carrying a pager, and I said what's that for, and he said, 'I'm waiting for a call.'

"He says: 'Why don't you do a drug deal?' And I said I just left the department. Tomorrow I'm flying out to San Diego. I'm going to manager's school. I said, 'Naw, I'm not going to do it.'"

"He said, 'Well, I'm waiting for a call. It's like a free deal.'"

Jimmy urged Torres to reconsider, telling him he was to buy ten ounces of cocaine for sixteen thousand dollars.

"I said, 'Well, I'm not a cop,'" Torres recalled. "He said, 'That's okay, your credibility is still there. What are they going to say? You're not a cop? Your credibility doesn't exist anymore?'

"I said, 'Jimmy, I got out for a reason, okay?' And I look back, and those were my last words to him. The reason I got out is…I got out because I lost somebody."

Torres, even though combat-toughened as a Marine infantryman in Vietnam, was dealing with his own issues. Three months earlier, his friend Ron Chelius, an undercover narc for the Nevada Department of Investigations, had been fatally shot while making a narcotics buy in Sacramento.

"Ron's death had a big impact on me, and I got out because I'd lost a friend. I didn't want to be a cop [anymore]."

Jimmy, focused on wrapping up his own stint as an undercover narcotics officer, went on to share some of the information about the pending transaction with Torres, and there was a suggestion he thought he was doing a one-on-one deal with Tom Wilson. Even if he had thought that the guy had an accomplice, Torres knew that Jimmy was "a scrapper" and one "hell of an athlete." He would be able to take care of himself, Torres figured. So, laden with his own concerns, he went to San Diego after the party, and Jimmy waited. Jimmy did not know he was walking into a "burn." He did not even have a gut instinct this time. Or if he did, he had too much guts.

Chapter 5

GETTING READY

With the plotting accomplished by both sides, the actual buy started on the morning of June 24, a Sunday. Tom Wilson placed his call to the RPD Narcotics Unit. It was the call Jimmy had waited for during the wedding festivities the night before. After some getting-to-know-you chat, Wilson offered to meet with Jimmy in the early afternoon to talk business. Not bashful, he made it clear that he needed to see if he could trust his new connect.

Jimmy agreed to meet with Wilson, alone. He consented to be scrutinized by the homeless, unemployed 20-year-old, one of the costs of doing business as an undercover narc.

Wilson set his trap, but clumsily. The meeting loomed as step two in his strategy to get the advantage. But a sharp hunger to make a quick strike clouded his vision. He saw through a green lens. His evil plan contemplated a target not associated with the law. First, he exposed his lair to his prey. Next, he failed to consider that the hunted was also the hunter, multiplied by ten. Jimmy was the hare to the hounds but those hounds were on a path to the wolf's den. Wilson schemed his way into certain failure.

Wilson, the pedestrian dealer of weed, saw himself as a real heavyweight and set out to sell that vision to his gang of youngsters. With Jimmy on the way, he invited Lani and Stites to take a berth on his boat to riches. The sting was on once his squad signed on. Olausen, already on board, prodded the recruits into action.

Lani and Stites, casino kitchen slaves, never dreamed of having a thousand dollars at one time. They decided to ditch work on the Sahara kitchen's swing shift that day. They didn't bother to call in sick.

Much later, Stites recalled, "I went to work every day except one day." His regret was apparent and pronounced.

Once convinced, the two new soldiers put their shoulders to the wheel. The never indecisive Lani pointed out the perfect place for the crime—an undeveloped weed and brush-covered section of riverbank close to the Riverside Convalescent Center, a repository for the dying old. It sat on the south bank of the river just past the west end of Idlewild Park. No one would see or hear them there, he was sure. The oldsters were out of it, blank-minded or enmeshed in their own nightmares. A skeleton nursing staff watching their snoring charges at midnight was far away and unconcerned. The doctors were all at home in bed at that hour. It was a perfect place. Greed bred perfect facts.

"There's an old building there," Lani revealed. "Like an old shithouse. There's some water pipes inside, and it's down a bank from the street. And you can't see through the trees from the street."

"Okay." Wilson savored the information. "Show us."

"Sure thing."

Wilson told Jimmy to meet him at midday at the El Tavern Motel, from where they would trip, all as a means of testing to see if Wilson could count on Jimmy's reliability as an honest drug buyer. At about two in the afternoon, Jimmy rolled into the El Tavern in his fiancée's "Z" car. The boys were watching from a window.

"That's gotta be him," Olausen said. "Check the dude out."

All four peered through the room's barely-cracked drapes as Jimmy parked in front of Room Nine, the room Stites and Lani rented.

"Don't look like no narc to me," Stites said.

"Me neither," Olausen agreed.

"How would you know?" Contempt flared in Wilson's voice. He and only he had experience with narcs. "Keep quiet. I'll check him out."

The other three stayed still as Wilson slid through the door and out into the midday sun. He greeted Jimmy and sidled up to the 280ZX, effecting an easy saunter.

Jimmy flipped his shades back a little and eyeballed the younger man. At that point, no lights went off. He half-leaned on the car for a moment, his long frizzy red hair looking anything but police-like, his eyes twinkling. After introductions were done, Wilson suggested that they go for a ride. Jimmy motioned to the passenger door with his head.

Jimmy, ever laid back and dressed for the occasion, didn't hurry. He stood in the warm sun, alert, ready—playing his part. This was the tough part, when the seller was intent on making sure he was not being set up by the cops. It was common for crooks to offer some dope to the potential buyer. Jimmy was not a smoker or a boozer, and he would talk his way out of taking a hit on a doobie when it was offered as a test to see if he was genuine. It would have been easy for him to inhale a little, and the fact that he wouldn't showed both courage and integrity. In fact, as Torres would remember later, "I'm trying to remember if I ever saw Jimmy drunk. He wasn't drinking a lot (at the wedding reception the night before) because of the deal that might go down."

Inside, Olausen, Stites and Lani talked a little about the possibility they were looking at a narc, but they quickly ruled it out. He didn't look like one. His orange blond hair, which had faded from the brilliant carrot of his boyhood, hung over his collar. He had long sideburns, and the ends of his reddish-brown Fu Manchu moustache drooped over the corners of his mouth and hung below his chin. He wore white Levi jeans, zip-up brown leather boots and a white T-shirt emblazoned across the front with "On a Scale of 1 to 10 I am a 10½." He wore a gold neck chain with a big cat claw charm hanging against his chest.

Wilson was right. Those three kids, sixteen to eighteen years old and barely out in the world, didn't really know what a narc looked like. Besides, Jimmy didn't look exactly healthy. He'd been working a lot of hours straight, not taking any significant break, and even attended the wedding reception with a phone in hand, ready to do the deal. He was tired; he was raspy.

Jimmy was a cop first and an actor second. He had his role down, the image mastered. He starred in the theater of illusions, where acting crossed into brutal reality. Jimmy fooled the marketers and consumers who believed they could see through his act. The Age of Aquarius became the time of "hey, we fooled you." Officer Hoff was a lead actor in a drama—a very high-stakes drama.

The best undercover buyers were regular-looking guys who did not stand out in a crowd. They avoided clothes and adornments that were out of the ordinary. The rule was, do not attract attention to yourself. Long hair and beards were okay because cops were typically short-haired and clean-shaven. Just like a good crook does not want to attract police attention, a good narc does not want to look different or be remembered. The big hat and shades at night may be cool on television but it does not work on the street.

How could those boys have spotted Jimmy the narc? They couldn't. They didn't. They weren't among the increasingly clever and streetwise. They didn't have the brain power or experience to make an informed evaluation regarding the key question—was he a narc? Fortune blurred the observations of the aspiring con men. Although a fool, Wilson did ensure that Jimmy did not have close contact with his backup officers when the deal went down. It was a clever ploy that would ruin many a life.

The boys did not sense the clear vision and smooth coordination of a rigorously trained and disciplined officer in Jimmy. They saw a party guy with long hair and drooping moustache. They did not detect the look of a cop, but they didn't really know what they were looking for. Thus assured, the four told themselves Jimmy couldn't be a narc. All they could see was his money—more money than any of them had ever touched.

Wilson got in the 280ZX. He gave instructions and Jimmy drove to the vicinity of Reno's Idlewild Park, the designated area for the "bunk sale."

The park embraces a section of the Truckee River about a mile west of the city's downtown core of casinos. On the river's south bank, mature pines, willows, cottonwoods and sycamores shade acres of mown grass. Gardens and small lakes attract strollers and a variety of structures offer shade for picnickers and facilities for meetings.

Jimmy, playing the role of dupe with cash and a serious need for artificial mood enhancement, followed Wilson's directions to cruise to the park and idle down its winding asphalt streets. There was no direction to drive to the undeveloped area at the park's west end, the site suggested by Lani for the deal. Jimmy's job was to keep Wilson thinking he had what Wilson wanted and that he trusted Wilson to produce what he wanted. His job was to let Wilson rehearse the deal and conclude he wasn't "the man."

Jimmy succeeded. Wilson was satisfied. Jimmy agreed to Wilson's conditions. If any early warning bells went off in his head, he took no heed. Misplaced trust and visions of glory do not promote clear thinking and sound tactical planning.

The two made a deal. Jimmy would get sixteen thousand in cash and, come midnight, hand it over to Wilson in return for ten ounces of coke. The exchange would be at a secret place still to be chosen in the park, Wilson said. He still had to get the final details and okay from his connection.

Wilson had been there—setting up a scam—before. Not at Idlewild Park but in the same role. Some two years earlier, he set up a burn in Sacramento that resulted in his arrest for robbery. That arrest was a learning experience for Wilson. He had been set up, but this time he intended to be creative. The Reno caper was going to be different because he'd make certain that the buyer was no cop. No backup meant no narc. From the start, he'd made it clear to Jimmy that only one person could be there as a buyer and one as a seller. Wilson would be alone and Jimmy was to come alone. That way, no one could interfere with the deal. One on one, no guns, no rip-offs, no cops—only illusions.

Wilson explained the reason for the one-on-one transaction to Jimmy in the car. It guaranteed that

Jimmy was neither a rip-off artist nor a cop. Wilson knew that cops worked in teams, had backup, and they liked controlled settings. There an even more important, albeit unvoiced reason: having Jimmy alone would allow Wilson to have full control given his support team of teenagers. Meanwhile, Jimmy had his team of ostensible heavyweights.

Wilson had it all orchestrated. He was not worried that Jimmy was a cop. He had ways to ensure that he wasn't. He would carefully avoid any possibility that Jimmy had help and guarantee that he was not walking into a trap.

He bought a box of baking soda and put one ounce each into ten separate zip-lock baggies. He then put the baggies of "bunk" into a duffle bag to take to the pump house, the chosen secret meeting place in the park, where he later concealed the baggies in the recesses.

At the El Tavern that afternoon, Wilson told the other three that he was concerned because Jimmy wouldn't smoke dope with him. Jimmy had some lodged behind his ear, Wilson said, but he didn't smoke. The boys, in an earlier bull session, had agreed that if Jimmy didn't smoke dope with them "he was a cop." Wilson covered that ground again. He quoted Jimmy as saying he was "allergic to dope." Wilson thought about that and concluded he must be the heat. Then he wavered, recanted and decided to go ahead with the scheme. "The money was too good," he later recalled.

As they concocted the plan for the big rip, Wilson and Olausen also made plans to split town after the scam went down. The plan was to take the money and head for Los Angeles, where they could get jobs in construction.

As the four would-be scammers talked, Jimmy drove back to police headquarters and laid out the details for his team. The sixteen thousand in buy money would go for the coke, which Jimmy quoted Wilson as saying would come from a larger batch that had been stolen from a police evidence locker, the site of which never was revealed. Further details, he said, would come in a phone contact about nine o'clock that night.

Jimmy arranged to use the "Z" car and made the other arrangements with the help of RPD staff. He cashed a check at a local casino to obtain the buy money. He had the buy money copied and he contacted his cover officers about the midnight ride that was about to begin.

The phone rang in the narcotics office a little later and Jimmy agreed to meet Wilson at the El Tavern at midnight. He and his surveillance team worked up a game plan to execute their undercover operation that night. Essentials included installing the wire in Jimmy's borrowed "Z" car. One of the uninvolved veteran officers with previous undercover experience in a large California city would later comment: "It was fucking stupid to wire the car instead of the cop just like it was just plain stupid to let Jimmy 'trip.'" The veteran ex-narc said that it may have been standard protocol at Reno PD but that did not "take the stink off it."

A cardinal rule in protecting the undercover buyer is never to let him "trip," that is, not to travel to an unplanned location. "Tripping" involves the undercover narc or snitch traveling to put a deal down where there is no cover. A narcotics unit that allows "tripping" risks losing contact with the narc or snitch, leaving him or her without cover. An undercover cop in this situation may find himself outnumbered and outgunned with no one to bail him out.

Since an undercover cop posing as a chump with a lot of money who's asking to be ripped off doesn't have the advantage of fear engendered by letting the peddlers know he is a cop—a member of the biggest, baddest gang in town—the surveillance team has to maintain control of each situation as it develops. One Brown-Hoff-Torres experience illustrates the point.

"Jimmy and I were doing a heroin buy at the parking lot at Keystone and Albertson's (supermarket) over there (near Idlewild Park)," Torres recounted. "I'll never forget this because we had brought in State Narcotics and one of my other best friends from the state was there. Rick was hiding in the back (of the supermarket). This guy was a wacko and I can't think of his name now, but there was this peddler for cocaine and heroin—or was it just heroin? So anyway, to make a long story short, we waited too long. Rick showed up and Jimmy said, 'Do you want to walk?' and Rick said, 'You don't want to walk?' Jimmy said, 'You just want to make contact and get out of there and we ended up waiting two hours.' The state guy said, 'You're going to end up getting somebody fucking killed and I don't want any part of this because they're in control of this, not you.' I say 'this is bullshit; let's get out of here. I don't want to be responsible for somebody's ass.' Then State Narcotics left. We waited.

"Rick says this guy is in the parking lot. He's coming. He's walking to us and I get out of the car. I went out and I grabbed him. We're going to just take him off. Screw it. Do the burglary (charge him with burglary) on a drugstore.

"I grabbed him and Jimmy came over and grabbed us both and threw us down. Jimmy reached under him and pulled a .38 out of his waistband. He just made a quick search and he happened to find a gun.

"You talk about you're going to get somebody killed one way or another. That was said to me in a rough way—to look back. You lose your control."

In short, the three rules to live by are:

- No tripping,
- Maintain visual contact of the undercover officer,
- And maintain audible contact.

Jimmy's squad would break all three rules that night.

Chapter 6

REAL PREPARATIONS

After Jimmy dropped Wilson back at the El Tavern, the four boys boozed, smoked dope and discussed the pending operation. They got high in the morning and stayed that way into the late night. They'd been high for days. The haze made them appreciate Wilson's brilliance.

Stites and Lani talked tough as they contemplated the large amount of cash. Their eyes got big and their heads buzzed when Wilson asked them to get in on the action.

Wilson told Lani and Stites he'd pay them thirty-five hundred dollars each for backing his play. They were in. They reviewed the plan, going over details. Euphoria kept the boys talking. Wilson kept them excited.

With the burn in mind, the four boys contemplated the site that Lani had proposed, the perfect spot in the tall trees and heavy brush near the river. Just to the west of the park, the distance between Idlewild Drive and the river narrowed to a small strip of river bend. There the road curved to the south and then back to the north, creating a blind spot.

As the street straightened for anyone driving west, it bordered the potential crime scene on the south. The river defined the northerly boundary and Idlewild Drive marked the south edge of the parcel. It was about a city block in size. Heavy stands of trees screened two sides of the plot from the park. On the third side of the rough triangle was the convalescent hospital, its back to the intended crime scene.

Olausen, Stites and Lani cut the thick brush, weeds and scrub willow to make blinds in which to hide. Later Wilson would bring Jimmy alone, unarmed and unsuspecting, "a babe in the woods."

The site was ideal. Besides being invisible from Idlewild Drive, the plot had access for vehicles via a cut in the curb. That cut led to a serpentine dirt road that wound through the trees and down an eight-foot embankment into the tangled pocket that formed the plot's floor. There stood the remnants of a tiny, ramshackle building that covered a concrete-lined hole in the ground. Ancient cast iron pipes had at one time carried water to valves in that hole. The "pump house" was Wilson's chosen spot for the burn.

The four decided on a stroll. They had to go out to a nearby supermarket to buy the bait, a box of baking soda to be packaged and sold to Jimmy, and they had to "scope out" their hiding spots. Just before the walk, Wilson telephoned Jimmy to confirm that the deal was on. Lani had heard about the burn a day earlier and the plan to kill Jimmy a few hours before the walk into the weeds. The teenager vacillated. He questioned the need to murder this stranger. Though no stranger to violence, he recoiled.

"Let's just knock him out," Lani suggested.

"No, there aren't going to be any witnesses," Wilson retorted.

The other boys did not object.

After buying the baking soda, the four trooped down to the river, crossed the Booth Street bridge and walked west on Idlewild about one-half mile to the ambush site. They stood in broad daylight, surveying the weeds and brush near the pump house. They were well concealed from any passing traffic. It was perfect.

Their reconnaissance over, the four turned back to their plan. They talked, smoked and drank until darkness ended the long afternoon. Summer solstice was gone but a few days. The sun stayed long in the west sky as they pondered. Eighteen-year-old Stites produced the tools of his trade, his personal set of chef knives—all long, professional grade, and sharp. He used a long, heavy sharpening steel to put a razor's edge on two of the knives in his kit.

Stites handed one knife to Lani and kept the other. Olausen had his own knife, a folding Buck. It was more than even a rancher's pocket knife. Its handle was brass and hardwood; its heavy single blade folded out, and once open, it locked in place, making it nearly as rigid as a military survival knife. The silver blade of tempered stainless steel was thick with ample curve for skinning large animals. The chiseled edge had been sharpened to slit the throat of the same large game. A strong sharp point made it an efficient stabbing tool.

Jimmy had spent two tours in the United States Army and was intimately familiar with knives, bayonets in particular. Although he had been trained to repel a knife attack, he knew the desperate move had small chance of success. As a street cop, he knew "not take a knife to a gunfight" or to go anywhere without a locked and loaded firearm. According to an ex-narc with extensive undercover experience, it was reckless and "felony stupid" to ever allow an undercover agent to go unarmed without both visual and audible contact. According to him, you better be "close enough to smell the crooks" if your partner is not armed. Jimmy's backup wouldn't even hear, let alone smell them.

As the night slowly drew close, both teams worked at getting up for their respective operations. Neither side could predict what would go down when the clash came and swords rattled. Even though the narcs all had experience as real street cops, it was yet to be seen who would react and how he would react.

In their deluded state, the four robbers' excitement grew and their judgment evaporated. They sprinkled their talk with tough words, working each other up for whatever the night would bring. That included the prospect that Jimmy might be a lot tougher than any of them and he might be "packing heat." He was and he wasn't, in that order.

Afternoon faded into evening and the four youngsters, their preparations and practice completed, kicked back to wait for midnight when Jimmy was to return with the money. Stites wrapped black electrical tape around the grip of his long butcher knife, and Olausen and Lani watched TV.

At the appointed hour, Stites, Lani and Olausen walked from their motel room toward the park. As they had earlier, they went east parallel to the river, over the bridge and west to the appointed site. It was roughly straight across the river from their motel room. There they would take up positions until Wilson would arrive with Jimmy. Their walk would be about two miles long, but the pump house was only about a quarter mile from the El Tavern. Had they wanted to, they could have waded across the wobbly stones on the river bottom and reached their destination in a few minutes. As it was, they were there in half an hour.

In time, they felt ready. Sunset came about eight-thirty, and to their advantage, there would be no moon that night. They put the baking soda and the three knives in a duffel bag and walked into the ever-darkening night. They concealed themselves in the Truckee's untended bushes they had cut and gathered earlier in the day, under little hollow haystacks, three separate camouflaged pockets. In those enclosures, the three expected to lie in wait, anticipating the arrival of Jimmy and Tom.

Wilson pronounced all in order and left, alone. His mission was to contact Jimmy and bring him back to his small band of armed desperados. Lani, Stites and Olausen stayed in their blinds, waiting for the cue, but not for long. They followed orders until fear and good sense overcame greed. They abandoned their posts and went back to the motel room. A collective faint heart nearly saved five lives.

At RPD, two miles down the river, Jimmy reported to the narcotics detail what he arranged with Wilson, a big buy, a record-setter for the section. Sergeant Rick Brown called in the cover officers. The Vice and Narcotics Details assembled and Downtown Brown gave the briefing. After the briefing, the cops turned to the actual preparation.

During the evening, Jimmy made a call to Anne Marie to tell her the deal was going down. She urged him to go easy on Wilson and Olausen. She never told him to protect himself.

Jimmy discussed how the matter should be handled with team member Gary Eubanks, who had already acquired the drug-use habit that would eventually blemish his career. Eubanks suggested that he accompany Jimmy in the role of bodyguard, but Jimmy nixed it. Wilson insisted that he not be accompanied by anyone. Besides, the 280ZX wasn't big enough to hold two officers and a "crook."

Officer Douglas installed the body wire under the driver's seat of the 280ZX, as opposed to putting it on Jimmy's person. The object was to pick up the voices in the car without putting the wire where Wilson might detect it. The device had a reliable range of a few blocks, and the custom was to listen on a hand-held receiver and record transmissions on a reel-to-reel recorder which was kept in a surveillance car. The officers believed that whatever went down would be in or involve the 280ZX, and they planned to listen in on what was said in the car and to keep the vehicle in their sights. This would be a tall order.

Historically, cars present problems. As a rule, police officers should not use their privately-owned vehicles on duty. A family car was all too often poorly suited to police work that might involve a pursuit. In 1979 Reno, however, practicality dictated that Jimmy Hoff and other officers in his unit use their own vehicles to successfully conceal their identities and carry out investigations. RPD command officers, like those in many other departments, looked at available cash and gave no priority to putting real undercover cars on the streets—cars that would fool their target *du jour.* There was one exception: the officers did rely on unmarked department vehicles to conduct long-range surveillance.

Undercover narcotics officers should know that when using their private cars in buys, they should not be faster than the surveillance cars. If a crook should manage somehow to get control of an officer's car, he shouldn't be able to outrun pursuing black and whites or unmarked police rigs. It was logical. And it was not taken into account.

Jimmy photocopied the one hundred and sixty C-notes that Sergeant Brown gave him. The team leader, with Chief Parker's okay, had gotten a city check issued to him on Friday, when the deal was originally contemplated. He cashed it at Harrah's Club at the start of the operation and returned with the cash to the Narcotics Office. Preparations ensued.

Rookie Deputy District Attorney Bruce Laxalt watched it go down, on hand because no buy and bust operation was ever routine. Each had the potential to take new twists, spawn new issues of law and require a quick, informed decision on how to strengthen the State's case. He was also there for backup. "We all had guns," he said of himself and other deputy prosecutors who assisted undercover cops. "We had weapons permits, and we were trained." Laxalt was also there because he loved the excitement. He wanted to be a "cowboy like Jimmy."

The rookie prosecutor said that Jimmy's buy from Wilson was "extremely well planned…very well planned." To him, it was adequate to place the body wire in the car to keep track of the operation, to photocopy the buy money and brief Jimmy and his six-member surveillance team. He did not mention the lack of weaponry and close cover. But he was a lawyer, not a cop or someone with combat experience or street moxie.

Jimmy, ever hip-cool and detached, sported his usual suppressed smile as money was photocopied.

One of the civilian personnel copied the money as Jimmy stood by. That employee, Debbie Ames, would write, 34 years later, the following:

Jimmy…where has all this time gone? I was one of the last to see you in the station that night as I photocopied the buy money for you. You were kidding around and flashing that great smile— you had no apparent concern about your job that fateful night. How could everything have gone so wrong? Here we are 34 years later and memories are as burned into my memory as ever. The James D. Hoff Memorial at Idlewild Park is my cover pic here on Facebook in your memory. It should never have happened…Rest well, my friend.
Signed: Debbie Ames, RPD Records Supervisor (1972-2003). June 26, 2013.

Ames finished photocopying the money and gave it to Jimmy, who put it in a green cloth bag. That bag had the outline of a marijuana leaf and the word *Stash* stenciled on it.

Brown confirmed that Jimmy got the cash and had it when he got into the 280ZX to make the buy.

At ten minutes to midnight, Reavis and Jimmy unloaded several items from Reavis' car into the 280ZX, which was parked outside the Public Safety Building. Included was a wooden box containing a scale that could be used to weigh narcotics. That went in back, through the rear hatch. Also in the car were some clothes and a plastic bag from the Sportsman sporting goods store. In the bag, underneath a few miscellaneous items, was Jimmy's .38 caliber revolver.

Reavis watched Jimmy put the gun in the car parked next to the three-story, hideous tan building that housed the Police Department, Jail and Municipal Court. The monolith stood on a triangular plot on the riverbank about two miles from Jimmy's destination that night.

In another move, license plates from Brown's unmarked RPD car, a Chevy Monte Carlo, were attached to the Z-car. That way, if the driver of any black and white saw the car, became suspicious for any reason and ran a license plate check by radio, the message back would be that it was Brown on a mission.

The sports car was very clean, gleaming on the outside, neat on the inside, and neither stained nor littered. Jimmy's ride ready, Reavis drove away in his personal car, taking up an assigned observation post near the Glory Hole, a bar on West Fourth Street about a mile west of the El Tavern Motel. There he could listen to the wire and radio traffic from other cars and start a moving surveillance. He could not observe Jimmy directly or provide immediate cover.

He was part of a tag team: six officers in six vehicles that would take turns tailing the Z-car in loose rotation. The idea was never to let Wilson see the same car in his area for very long. One surveillance car would follow for a while, then drop back and be replaced by another that had been moving the same direction but a block over. They coordinated by radio. Drop, follow, drop back.

While near the Glory Hole restaurant, Reavis had his police radio going and heard Douglas, on a frequency other than the one the body wire was set to broadcast on, say, "Tell Ricky Brown that he and Jimmy had checked the 'bug' and that it was functioning."

Jimmy and Douglas checked the transmitter as Jimmy drove toward the El Tavern some eight minutes after midnight. He turned the wire on and drove past Douglas, asking him if he could hear him. "Flash your lights if you hear me," he said. Douglas, at Ben's Liquor Store at Fourth and Keystone, heard him and flashed his lights. Douglas said that after his initial test of the "wire" with Jimmy, he heard nothing from it but "squelch" noise. He expected to hear voice traffic but did not.

"I suspected a malfunction," he later recalled. If such a suspicion existed, it was not shared. He did not air his concern to Sergeant Brown or any surveillance team members during the intended buy/bust. Nor did he act to halt the deal or warn Jimmy, who would have no way of knowing if there was a malfunction.

Wilson took his first stab at the deal after leaving his crew ensconced in the weeds. Alone, Jimmy drove to the pickup point. Wilson joined him and they took a meandering course about the streets of Southwest Reno which allowed Wilson to look for a tail. Satisfied, Wilson instructed Jimmy to pull onto the dirt road and wait while he made sure the dope was in place. He exited the car and walked into the trees. When he returned, the 280ZX started up again, rolled out of the trees and took a circuitous route back to the El Tavern. This time, the narcs were watching. Wilson had just discovered that his gang had abandoned their hiding spots and returned to the room.

At the motel, Wilson leapt from the Z-car and charged inside one of the rooms where he soundly berated his fainthearted accomplices, castigating them for running from the scene. The three younger boys protested that it was "a setup."

"Come on, let's go," Wilson ordered, unimpressed by their arguments. "You can't back out now. Get back to the river."

Wilson also looked scared and told them that Jimmy had a gun and was "going to kill me."

Then Jimmy yelled from the car. "We're going to do this thing now," Olausen remembered him exclaiming. "I'm getting tired of this bullshit."

Gambling that his tune-up had worked, Wilson told his cohorts he would be there shortly—after he took Jimmy on a wild goose chase to give them time to set up again.

Douglas had been in position to see the 280ZX pull into the motel and park away from Lani and Stites's room. Minutes later, he saw Wilson emerge from the other side of the motel, moving excitedly and waving his arm and pointing, talking to someone inside. Jimmy could not see Wilson from his vantage point in the car. He was also too far away to hear the conversation in the room. When Wilson slid back inside the car with Jimmy, the two took off. Douglas expressed no concern that Wilson had talked to another person or persons. The clues were piling up but not for the clueless. It was Jimmy's deal, and J.D. stayed cool, apparently very detached—or unconscious.

As the Z-car pulled away from the El Tavern the second time, surveillance followed. No cop stayed behind to check out the motel, to see who was inside or see who came out and where they went. Douglas did see three people walking beneath the nearby train trestle onto Second Street toward Idlewild Park a few minutes later. He did not appreciate what he saw: three teenagers who were Wilson's backup team creeping back to the river, their knives in a duffel bag carried by Olausen.

"When we went back there, we were scared. We were helping Tom out because he was scared," Olausen said later. "I owed him money."

While his gang set up the second time, Wilson and Jimmy traveled across town to finish setting up the deal because something went wrong down by the river.

Reportedly, the listening device was working again as Jimmy listened to the explanation. Exactly what was said on the trip is yet unknown because the cops claim the tape was "lost." While the cover officers conducted a rolling surveillance, Jimmy drove south with Wilson to a large apartment complex some three miles south of the downtown area that was well known to local law enforcement. In 1979, police dispatch policy required that two officers be sent on all calls for service to the Robin Hood Apartments. It was a good spot to "cop some dope" or get in a fight.

Jimmy waited in the car while Wilson went into the complex to contact his mythical "connect." He allowed sufficient time for his teenage accomplices to get in their hiding places and then told Jimmy to drive back to the park.

At 1:24 a.m., Sergeant Brown saw Jimmy driving north with his passenger.

Wilson, with his teenage backups in place, directed Jimmy to the tree-shrouded area of brush by the river again. The darkened street ran east and west, and Wilson had Jimmy pull off on the north side, nosing the sports car onto what appeared to be an abandoned driveway out of view of passing traffic. That concealed parking spot was where Brown and Reavis had earlier seen Wilson in the pale glow of the Z-car's dome light. This time, Jimmy, without cover followed Wilson into the trees. He would not walk back out.

Chapter 7

HE'S ALIVE?

En route from the murder scene to the burial site, one of three things occurred. Wilson, Olausen or Lani stabbed the living, breathing Officer Hoff several more times through the bed sheet in which he was wrapped. At least this is the account that the cops and prosecutors would run with despite several early official statements to the contrary. Or, an overactive imagination drove one of them to mutilate a dead man with additional punctures. The third possibility, asserted by Lani and Stites, is that all the wounds were inflicted at the original crime scene when the prospect of possible knife play drove them to practice their knife wielding on a mattress covered with what was to become Jimmy's shroud. The truth of their assertion was to become critical, but the target mattress was not preserved after the fact so their explanation could be neither verified nor debunked.

The true version of events will take years to discern and may never be revealed. What is certain is that a transmitter in the car was working at least part of the time, with the signal from that Kel unit being recorded. The tape, however, "went missing." Such was the nature of justice in Nevada in the twentieth century. Such is the nature of justice in Nevada today.

Between the shrouding of the body, dead or alive, and the arrival of the Z-car in Dog Valley, California, there is only speculation as to what happened. Much was to be made of the activity in those cramped quarters of the car.

When the makeshift hearse left the El Tavern parking lot, the boys didn't know the car had been seen entering and leaving the El Tavern parking lot and that they were being followed. Wilson lead-footed it when he aimed the 280ZX out of the El Tavern's horseshoe parking lot and onto Fourth. Illogically, the maneuver bespoke a wish to draw attention to himself.

Wilson accelerated hard on Fourth Street toward the intersection with Interstate 80 and shot west to the nearby California Sierras. The surveillance team, in their relatively slow tubs, followed but lost the race. Jimmy's car caromed out of sight. Brown's men watched as the 280ZX sprinted away. That signaled trouble—Jimmy alone wouldn't be splitting like that.

Team members got onto the interstate behind the 280ZX struggling to keep up. They followed the tail lights, losing ground by the second. They completely lost sight of the Z-car close to Boomtown Casino and Resort near the California state line.

Officer Douglas, who was initially ahead of the 280ZX, watched it in his rear-view mirror as it exited onto Exit 5, about seven miles from downtown Reno. He made a quick U-turn in the freeway median and shot back to the exit but by that time the sports car had disappeared. Douglas chose not to call for uniform assistance. Why there was no call for uniform or outside agency assistance may never be addressed.

Exit 5 takes traffic onto old U.S. 40 about a mile east of the Boomtown Casino and Hotel complex and into a small, idyllic community in the sparse pines on the eastern side of the Sierra. The town is named Verdi, after Italian composer Giuseppe Verdi. Locals pronounce their town's name VUHR—die.

While the freeway crosscuts due west into the foothills, the old road tracks the river channel and leads through Verdi and into Dog Valley, home to mule deer, rabbits, coyotes, mountain lions and an occasional bear. The surveillance team, except for Douglas, had gotten so far back they didn't see the sports car make the turn. They were on the road to

California, driving toward Sacramento and San Francisco. Logic indicated that Wilson and his companions were fleeing the state. Blind, the backup officers drove right past the old U.S. 40 turn. They'd lost Jimmy. No one called for help. Only much later would the alarm sound. They made no attempt to enlist all available resources to save Jimmy. At that hour there were several agencies with uniformed officers available on both sides of the state line. No one asked for assistance from the Nevada Highway Patrol or the California Highway Patrol, both of which worked Interstate 80 as it left Nevada and headed into the mountains on the California side.

Sergeant Reavis sped toward Verdi in his unmarked surveillance vehicle. He saw the 280ZX on Interstate 80 closing on the California border. He spotted the smaller car at an intersection, but by the time he could slow and turn around, it was gone. He continued to roam and search, fruitlessly. He was not ready to call for assistance.

After Wilson made his turn off the interstate, he followed old U.S. 40 into town and past the community post office, a couple of closed bars and a restaurant. He continued west on the old highway then turned north onto Dog Valley Road which led into California.

He had to slow in the darkness as his headlights searched out the curves of the paved but narrow two-lane road. He wound past a darkened elementary school, dipped down onto an ancient bridge to cross the Truckee River again and passed a timeworn cemetery. Ornate tombstones stood tall, overlooking the quiet highway.

The road straightened some, and Wilson sped up a little to cross a wide part of the valley and entered a mountainous area. That was where they searched for a burial plot for the now certainly dead Jimmy. Riddled with stab wounds, he was but a link to be concealed, a link that waited to come back from a grave not yet selected, a corpse that waited to haunt them. Wilson and his boys carried the carcass where tall pines and meadows were only interrupted by narrow streams and dirt roads, where few people passed.

The burial venue, Dog Valley, was frequented by local woodcutters, rock hounds digging for quartz crystals and fishermen looking for elusive brook trout in dinky streams. That night few of the seldom-used camping spots were inhabited by outdoor types in tents, and none were disturbed by Olausen, Lani and Wilson carrying the body of Jimmy Hoff.

Rigor mortis came quickly to the corpse, quickly enough to complicate burial. The onset of rigor mortis is a very poor indicator of when life fled from a departing unfortunate because of variables. It's caused by bodily chemical processes that change in the body at the time blood stops flowing. The norm is two to four hours after death with full development in six to twelve hours.

Among known factors that accelerate rigor are heavy exercise, severe convulsions and violent muscular exertion just before death. At least two of those factors were present in Jimmy's death. It was likely that his body stiffened quickly.

Besides rigor mortis, there is also liver mortis to consider. This condition is noted by discoloration in the lower part of a corpse within hours of death. The presence of liver mortis may indicate what position a body was in at the time immediately following death and whether the body was moved after death. Although critical, there is no indication in the record as to the presence of liver mortis.

The killers had come to the burial site unprepared. They stopped by a mound of dirt and tried to dig a hole. They were without tools. They had neither shovel nor pick. Worse, the corpse could not be folded into a compact package of dead bone and tissue. A long, odd-shaped grave was needed. They got back in the car and drove off to look for softer dirt. They didn't find softer dirt but they found a more accommodating place: a culvert along the gravel highway.

Wilson and Olausen stuffed the sheet-clad body into the culvert's opening, leaving the feet and legs to protrude. Lani refused to help, or even look. The killers tried but couldn't stuff Jimmy's body all the way into the straight metal tube which had a diameter of eighteen inches.

They shoved the body partway into the culvert and hastily threw rocks onto the legs and feet, leaving one brown shoe visible to an alert passerby. That oversight became very significant some hours later. It would become an important factor with the cops and prosecutors.

The killers' hasty burial of Officer Hoff did not go completely unnoticed. One of the campers in the area came forward later. That camper got up early and began his drive to work about 3:00 a.m. As he wound down Dog Valley Road he saw "a Datsun sports car, dark in color, he thought it was red, parked on the west side of the road." The Z-car was perpendicular to his line of travel. The camper's headlights swept across the car and revealed one person was walking toward the car. He described him as a "dark-complected man, average height, average weight of maybe 170 pounds. He had hair covering his ears, a little in the style of an Afro cut, and maybe a mustache."

The three killers finished their grisly job of disposal, got back in the bloodied car and headed back to the motel. As they approached Interstate 80, they noticed several police cars traveling west at high speed.

Ironically, Sergeant Reavis spotted them again. At that point, he and Douglas had come together, and from the area of Hill Street he saw the little black car spin off Verdi's Third Street and shoot back toward the freeway. They were not able to catch up. Again, they did not alert the uniformed officers.

As they made their way back to Reno, hard-charging Brown took a distant position. From radio traffic, he learned that the 280ZX had gone to Verdi. He didn't drive to Verdi. Still in Reno, he saw the 280ZX leave the interstate at the Keystone off-ramp at 3:26 a.m. He didn't follow it to the El Tavern. He did not trace the occupants. He did nothing. Perhaps the "Buds" had deadened his reasoning powers. Perhaps he was suspecting the worst and was locking up mentally.

Wilson, Olausen and Lani gradually realized that there were a lot of cop cars buzzing around like angry hornets. It was time to lose Jimmy's car. They arrived at the El Tavern about one hour and ten minutes after they had left, around 3:30 in the morning. Dawn was not much more than an hour away.

Officer Atyeo, still in position at the Silver State Motor Lodge across from the El Tavern, saw the 280ZX return at 3:28 a.m. It drove to the rear of the motel and two people got out and headed toward the building. Then a third exited and ran to catch up with the others. The three rounded a corner and went out of sight.

Atyeo continued to watch the El Tavern from a distance as the four killers carried a variety of items from Room Nine to Jimmy's car. Those individuals came around the corner from the motel and crammed bundles and suitcases into the back of the 280ZX. The car, containing four persons, followed the alley back to Fourth Street. Atyeo did not see Jimmy. He just watched. He did not alert the troops and did not approach.

The boys were now bent on escape. Stites didn't want to run but consented to leave after Olausen persuaded him that the police were onto them. They left with Wilson at the wheel of the Z-car, Olausen in the passenger seat with Stites in his lap, and Lani in the blood-stained back of the car. They'd only gone a short distance when they saw a trucker using a walkie-talkie. Olausen later claimed that he counseled the others to turn themselves in but Wilson said no and kept driving.

"You really didn't know who was after you, so there was some fear there," Olausen would recall long afterward. "It was just running from everybody. This was two or three in the morning. There was a trail on the car."

As this conversation went on, Atyeo ran to his car, took Cemetery Road behind the trailer park to Stoker Street and onto Fourth Street.

"Just as I reached Stoker, they came up at a high rate of speed, almost sliding into my car, pulled back into Cemetery Road, went past me in the other direction and back to the trailer park." Atyeo said. He lost them from that point.

The four, doubling back to the east, hid the car behind the Silver Lake Lodge on West Fourth about a quarter mile from the El Tavern and fled on foot. They stopped for a minute or so on a nearby hill, and Wilson doled out money to Lani and Stites, twenty-five hundred together. After getting their cash, Lani and Stites split off from Wilson and Olausen, going their separate ways. Still in the 280ZX were their two suitcases, a duffel bag and clothing bundled in an El Tavern bed sheet—a mountain of incriminating evidence. Contents included Wilson's and Olausen's clothes and personal effects, the baking soda, ID cards belonging to Lani and Stites, Jimmy's guns, and a set of nunchucks (a martial arts weapon made up of two sticks connected at one end by a short chain or rope). There was no money.

By that time, four o'clock or so, Brown and his team realized that they were in big trouble and that Jimmy, if he was still alive, was in a major predicament. Brown called Chief Parker, and the Nevada Highway Patrol was alerted, as was the Washoe County Sheriff's Office. All of Reno's on-duty cops were on notice and every narc from the other local agencies was put on alert and called out to look for Jimmy. One of the alerted officers had reported seeing the 280ZX heading back toward Reno and an all-out search had been initiated for the car and its occupant.

Officer John Poirier eased his white patrol car down the back streets in the vicinity of Keystone and El Tavern motel. He found the 280ZX just minutes after the boys had fled from it. It sat abandoned in a field northeast of the Silver State Lodge Motel in the 1700 block of West Fourth. He radioed his find to Police Dispatch and anyone listening.

The information was relayed to Chief Parker. He pulled on jeans and a red checked shirt and headed for the area of the car. At the same time, young officer Ed Takach was in the neighborhood working patrol on the midnight shift. He left his patrol car and was checking the mobile home park at the rear of the El Tavern. He suddenly confronted Wilson and Olausen. Three sets of eyes got big as they faced off for an interminable second-and-a-half. Wilson and Olausen were now the hunted. As he faced the "armed and dangerous" youths, Takach reached for his .357 revolver. Pure instinct directed the gun to their common eye level. The prey faced a looming six inches of gun barrel. Wilson and Olausen ran in opposite directions.

As Olausen ran, he ditched his Buck knife in one of the small yards adjacent to one of the mobile homes. He and Wilson ran hard in the darkness with speed that fear lent to their young legs.

Ed Takach wasn't much older than the two young killers but his speed didn't approach theirs. He pursued tentatively with the caution expected of an officer chasing two possible killers around corners and into the darkness. The two fugitives soon met up near a brush-covered ditch which fed irrigation water to the local farmers. Takach didn't find the two boys, but he did find Olausen's Buck knife about an hour later.

Wilson and Olausen ran a short distance to escape. Satisfied they were not followed into the high brush, they hunkered down. Out of wind, they stopped less than two hundred yards from where they had abandoned the 280ZX. Their victim, the dope dealer, had attracted inordinate attention. It would later dawn on them that he was instead a brother officer to their blue-suited hunters.

Wilson and Olausen had no idea that they'd been under sporadic, long range surveillance for almost a day. They didn't connect the patrol cars they saw on the freeway with themselves and the pimp/dealer they'd just buried. The brief face-off they had with Takach seemed but a freak happening. Not understanding that they were the object of a deadly manhunt, a gathering force like a furious hurricane on the horizon, they settled down in an uncultivated area of dry ditches, blue-green sagebrush and rabbit weed just north of Fourth Street. Having found a small open area surrounded by high brush they rested on the cool sandy earth. Sleep came as only the young and tired can experience it. No fear visited their dreams as they dozed in the dry ditch. They seemed well concealed not far from the riverbank where Jimmy's blood dried in the coming dawn.

The two desperados slept through the morning until they thought it would be safe to slink out of the field where they lay. Newly wealthy, they faced the prospect of unexpected pleasures. Who could miss the foolish dope dealer?

Chapter 8

THE LAWYERS

While the manhunt was still in progress and with dread that Jimmy was dead or dying, the top brass in the District Attorney's office put themselves on priority standby. District Attorney Calvin R. X. Dunlap was out of town so Chief Criminal Deputy D.A. Mills Lane stepped in to supervise.

"Word came to us that there was a narcotics operation that may have gone awry," Lane recalled. As the first assistant to the D.A. and an aggressive 42-year-old Marine Corps product, he set up tight communications with RPD headquarters.

Deputy Laxalt had begun work on the case, obtained the search warrant and helped execute it, but it was Lane who would call the shots from the first arrests forward. After all, he had known Jimmy since he was a blue suit pushing a patrol unit on the streets of Reno. Lane liked the young officer a lot.

"He was a good-looking young man, and I'd had him as a witness in trials," Lane said later. "He was always prepared."

And when Jimmy was gone, lost while tripping, Lane was concerned.

"It was bedlam at the cop shop," Laxalt said of the situation he saw after returning to the police headquarters from Verdi. Wilson and Olausen had just been arrested after they were found and arrested where they slept, and Lane had been notified.

"I recall them being hustled in, and they went into a little conference room," Laxalt said. "My involvement at that point was over. I recall Mills storming in very soon after, and there was a big debate. I was off the case."

Laxalt deferred readily, in part because of his pup status in the D.A.'s office but more so because he knew why: "Mills knew Jimmy …he was too close to Jimmy…I have to believe that Mills and Cal (D.A. Dunlap, Lane's boss) were both very close to him."

Mills was already something of a town hero, an irascible charmer and a gruff talker whose features revealed he once did some serious boxing. Lane hurried to check on the suspects when he learned of their arrests. No greenhorn, Lane had become a deputy district attorney eight years earlier. As a prosecutor, Lane had convicted twenty-two murderers in sixteen separate cases, and he viewed himself as a self-professed and rigid adherent to the Western philosophy of good versus evil. He was also a strong proponent of the death penalty. Besides his diligence and strict view of right and wrong, he had another attribute—that of an astute poker player who knew how to read faces.

First he went to the county jail on the west side of Reno's historic limestone courthouse and downstairs from the D.A.'s office to see what he could learn from Wilson about Jimmy's whereabouts and condition.

"Basically, Wilson told us to fuck off," Lane said. "You could forget Wilson."

Lane didn't pursue the gang leader and instead went to police headquarters to check out Olausen.

"Olausen was scared to death," Lane said.

The boy had good reason to be scared. He was starting to understand that even though he had not personally killed Jimmy, he was looking at a first-degree murder charge because of conspiracy laws and the "felony-murder rule." That rule, a principle going back to the common law, is that one who causes death in the commission of a felony—even without intending it—is guilty of murder.

Olausen's youth and fear gave Lane a possible advantage. He had the police detectives introduce him.

The strategy to separate Wilson and Olausen had formed quickly, and word of their arrest hit the airwaves with equal speed. That word was not lost on Fred Hill Atcheson, a self-described "news junkie" working in the Public Defender's Office. He'd been a lawyer since 1976, and defending indigents was his first job. That day, his lunch over, he was driving to his office on Center Street when he heard a broadcast about the killing and the capture of two youthful suspects.

"I knew they'd be in one of two places," Atcheson said. "My office was downtown. I went to the Sheriff's Office in the old courthouse to see whichever one was there."

Atcheson already suspected that the two would be quickly separated based on his two-and-a-half years defending the criminally accused. He knew that the police had a set of standard procedures and this was one of them.

"Tom Wilson was there," he said. "I talked briefly to him and told him not to make any deals and that if he did it probably wouldn't be binding.

"I became aware that the other guy was over at the Reno city jail…This case had death penalty written all over it. I went to the city jail (upstairs at the police station)."

A vigorous six-footer in a hurry, Atcheson parked outside the dry-mud-colored concrete edifice housing the police headquarters, took the elevator up one floor and ignored the dirty-feet smell coming from the crowded cells. He strode to a high counter where two jailers waited and asked for Olausen, thinking of himself as a man with a mission.

"I considered myself a veteran, and I was the chief trial attorney for the Public Defender," he said. "I had had a lot of tough cases with the D.A.'s office, and they played hardball at all times. They didn't give you any discovery. They didn't give you any witness statements. It was a hell of a way to get trained."

Atcheson found the police too would play hardball on that Monday, especially against him.

"There was a lot of hostility that day," he remembered. "There was no joking." They got him out placing him with Atcheson in a tiny interview room set aside for attorneys. He was in a jump suit, and he looked terrified—just scared.

"I just introduced myself and I said that it was pretty important for him not to talk to anybody at this time."

Atcheson had barely started speaking when, as he later recounted: "And then, boom, the door opened up and a uniformed cop said I'd have to leave. There were two of them."

"I said, 'What do you mean?'"

"He said, 'Mills Lane said you have to leave.'"

Atcheson protested but it did no good.

"I was basically escorted out of the room," he said. "There were two cops, one on each arm. They just took me out, and I was pretty mad because I knew I had the authority to be there. There was a statute."

But statute or not, the uniforms did as they'd been told, never allowing Olausen the chance to agree to be represented by the Public Defender's Office.

"I said, 'I'll be back,'" Atcheson said dryly, two decades later. "I said, 'I don't want anyone talking to him. Do you understand me?' They just gave me a bum's rush."

Olausen remembered his separation from the deputy public defender more colorfully.

"He was going to give me instruction on my rights," Olausen said. "I told him these guys are trying to kill me, and Fred says, 'You're all right now.'"

Olausen remembered that hadn't been true. "In almost no time, two officers kicked the door open and said, 'What the fuck are you doing here?'

"'Hey, I'm the public defender." Olausen remembered the answer the slender Atcheson gave, and he remembered the response.

"No, you're leaving or we're dragging you out."

"He's my client," Atcheson reportedly said.

"Are you fucking deaf?"

"I'm not leaving," the public defender responded, according to Olausen.

"They grabbed him," he recalled. "I remember him yelling, 'This is outrageous...you can't do this...this is illegal.'"

At that juncture, Atcheson was left with only his legal recourse. Other than turning his back, he had no option but to return to his office and slam together an emergency motion: a request for a court order to give him access to Olausen.

Lane, more oriented to results than form or theory, gave top priority to getting Jimmy back alive. He held out no realistic hope but innately knew that anything and everything had to be done. He too was of the brotherhood. Jimmy had been betrayed once but he would not be betrayed by Mills Lane. With only a slim chance to save Jimmy, Mills marched on. Once a Marine, always a Marine. He assessed the suspects' faces and demeanors. He had seen in Olausen an uncertain, scared and perhaps wanting-to-be-helpful attitude. Lane, who made it obvious that he did not hold the criminal defense bar in high regard and publicly stated when asked about a particular defense lawyer that he "wouldn't piss on her if she was on fire," was not to be interfered with by any criminal defense attorney.

As an arrestee, Olausen was entitled to a phone call. He did not get it but someone in the RPD called his father, John, at his home in Chico to inform him that his son was in the worst of trouble. "I think it was Steve's one phone call," John remembered later. Olausen disagreed, saying someone else made the call. John Olausen, an amputee with one leg and a need for support, enlisted his brother Richard to drive him. The two headed over the Sierras toward Reno immediately. They had to travel about one hundred eighty miles, much of it on secondary highways, to get to Reno. It took nearly three hours to get there.

In Reno when the NDI agents Gates and Drew laid hands on Wilson and Olausen, the two candidates for the gas chamber ceased being partners. No one had to tell them that he who could blame the other for the killing of Jimmy Hoff could put a little distance between himself and the green, octagonal death room.

The same two officers who had ejected Atcheson returned to Olausen.

"They roughed me up for talking to him (Atcheson). They socked me in the stomach and the solar plexus—just a wakeup. I couldn't breathe. 'If you're going to stay alive, you better know who the fuck you're dealing with,' (they said) and they dragged me to an interrogation room."

That conference room was in the Detective Division, one floor below and down a long hallway on the main floor. Atcheson was not there. Detectives Bob Penegore and Wayne Teglia were waiting along with Mills Lane. Businesslike but not physical, the detectives wasted no time going to work on the 18-year-old.

"Mills identified himself and said that they wanted to ask questions," Olausen said. "He said he was the only one who could help me and asked me how (he could do it). I said he (the escorting officer) is trying to kill me."

Lane listened intently. Intent but impatient, he locked eyes with Olausen across a well-worn, hardwood conference table.

"There was a little bit of cat and mouse, and we asked him where Hoff was," Lane said years later. "He didn't say anything. We said, 'If you tell us where Jimmy is we won't go for the death penalty.'"

Lane admonished the youngster about his right to an attorney and that anything "you say will be used against you." He also got what he regarded as a sufficient waiver of those rights. He had a deal in mind for Olausen—a bargain. He would insulate Olausen from the gas chamber if Olausen would help him find Jimmy, who might be alive.

"I'm the D.A. and I can do this," the feisty prosecutor said.

"I told him I wanted to talk to an attorney," Olausen said.

"He said okay after this interview, and I also said I wanted to talk to a Mormon bishop. He told me that they would do that. He left and Eubanks came in and told me, 'You're going to be smart or you're not going to make it.'

"Mills Lane came back in with a fast food hamburger and a soda and put it on the table. He told me, 'If you're hungry we've got something for you to eat but we want to talk to you first.'"

Olausen did wind up talking, but mostly to the detectives. Lane, having perhaps his biggest case ever in his hands, knew he could wind up being a witness—not a state's attorney—if he did too much of the interrogation. He hung back most of the time while Penegor and Teglia leaned on Olausen, bargaining to find Jimmy. It was a "Mutt and Jeff" operation, with Penegor playing the heavy and Teglia the nice guy.

By then Olausen's father had joined them. "Penegor was pretty hostile," the elder Olausen recalled. He witnessed the latter part of his son's questioning after the long drive over the Sierras. "Teglia was the good guy." What he did not know was that Penegor was not acting. It was whispered, not around him, that he was "one ruthless son of a bitch." The stories of several bad guys going down, victims of his deadly aim, were often repeated around RPD. Of course, they were "justified shootings."

The technique worked. Both Olausens, father and son, weakened.

"They brought in my high school yearbook," Steve Olausen said. "I was a junior in high school...Pleasant Valley in Chico. They handed me the book and started pointing out my best friend and said, 'Do you know him?' and I started crying...also pictures of me in sporting events and wrestling. They're telling me, 'You're in a lot of trouble, and you can fix it.' It pissed me off and I said, 'I'm not talking.'"

The detectives did not give up.

"Then they brought in a preacher guy. I still have his card. I asked, 'Are you Mormon?' He said, 'No, but I'm just as good as a Mormon.' He started interrogating me. I'm not saying nothing. I wanted an attorney. They'd already beat up the attorney

(Atcheson). They said, 'you did have an attorney, and look what we did to his ass.' Mills Lane said that. Then he said, 'I'm going to let you have a private conversation with this guy.' He starts interrogating. 'Did you leave Jimmy up there?' And I'm saying, 'I don't want to...I want to talk to my dad...an attorney.' He kept interrogating...'I don't want to talk any more.'"

Although Lane would later assert that no information that the suspect made to the clergyman was relayed in any manner to any agents of the state, as Olausen remembered the interrogation and involvement with the clergyman, Lane returned after a few minutes and behaved as though Olausen had agreed to cooperate in taking Lane to where Jimmy's body lay.

"He told me I'd get four years in a boys' camp (if I cooperated)," Olausen said of Lane. "This was after they told me that I'd face the death penalty."

In another ploy, or maybe an unintended happenstance, some officers were overheard by John and Richard Olausen saying that they were going to kill Olausen. Richard looked like a law enforcement officer, and perhaps some RPD members didn't realize he was part of the Olausen family when they vented their rage. More likely, in Olausen's words:

"They told Dad they couldn't guarantee my security, and Dad signed a waiver as a guardian.

"Dad basically told me that he thought that they were going to kill me, and basically he told me to tell the whole truth. I understand why he did what he did."

Meanwhile, Defense Attorney Atcheson completed his emergency motion and contacted District Court Judge John Gabrielli for an expedited hearing. He also called Chief Deputy Lane.

Gabrielli served as a presiding judge and handled matters that hadn't been assigned to other judges.

"I saw him virtually right away, got hold of Mills and told him I was going to meet with the judge. I told (the judge) the story. Mills was there. Mills said, 'He's right, judge, I'm wrong. I shouldn't have done that...I overstepped my bounds, and I won't do it again.'"

"I got the order from the presiding judge that I shall be allowed immediate access to Steven Olausen," Atcheson said. "I went back to the jail feeling bright with the power in my briefcase.

"When I got there, they were no longer in the jail section. They were in the Detective Division, and Olausen was back in one of the interview rooms."

It was between 3:30 and 4:00 p.m. Atcheson's way was blocked by a receptionist and an array of desks. He asked an officer to let him into the area.

"I was informed that Olausen no longer desired to speak to me in spite of the power percolating in my briefcase," Atcheson said. "I didn't necessarily believe it and said I wanted to talk to him. The officer said, 'I'll ask him.' He returned with John Olausen, a nice guy. He looked like his kid. He was devastated. He said they had it all worked out.

"I talked to John and he said everything was just hunky-dory. You could tell he was very upset. I don't think I had anything to do with Olausen after that."

The senior John Olausen had witnessed a good deal of the bargaining and questioning in the interrogation room and said later that his son made two significant statements. First, he confirmed what the officers already knew—that he had been with Wilson, Stites and Lani. Second, he confessed that he had helped move Jimmy and knew where he was. He agreed, in return for immunity from the death penalty, to take officers to the location.

John Olausen said that Lane stayed out of the interrogation room and the statement given by his son was taped. Olausen did not waive his rights to an attorney, his father said, but he did tell how the stabbing incident started, how "the officer lost control," who was there and where Jimmy was. John Olausen also said he'd been told that Wilson told officers he "didn't know anything about anything" and had not been at the stabbing scene.

The younger Olausen claimed that no killing had ever been intended; that while down at the pump house, Jimmy had gotten out of control and had grabbed Wilson. Wrestling ensued and Jimmy tried to break for the car and the bag that contained his gun. Wilson screamed, "He's got a gun, he's got a gun." That was "when Lani nailed him." Olausen denied any stabbing, and years later his father would believe that Lani's blow was the fatal one even though later evidence would refute that. Of immediate significance, however, was Olausen's statement regarding Jimmy's location.

"Once he said I'll take you to where he's at, we said let's go," Lane said.

Steve Olausen then left the interview room and got into a police car in the belief he had made his own deal with Lane to escape any possible death sentence. "He was all happy," he said of Lane, "and he said four years in boys' camp."

Making the deal didn't come easy for Lane.

"I'm a death penalty advocate," he said later. "I believe in the death penalty, but the deal was made. We made the deal."

Lane was to confirm in court proceedings later that he had made Olausen an offer that the Office of the District Attorney would not seek the death penalty for Olausen if he showed the police where Hoff had been left. Lane did not mince words or soften the effect of what he clearly believed was "a deal." His word was his bond.

Olausen hesitated only briefly before agreeing to the deal. As he saw it, his promise made the gas chamber go away. He was 18 years old and had no attorney beside him but he had been made to fully understand how much trouble he'd gotten into.

Handcuffed and wearing shackles, he got into the police car for a ride to Verdi. He took comfort in having done what was necessary to escape the gas chamber. That comfort would dissipate later. He, like Atcheson, would have reason for cynicism. The public defender would say in print, "I requested and was given an expedited conference with former Judge John Gabrielli attended by Mills Lane. Mills acknowledged that Nevada law allowed access to the jail by members of the Public Defender's Office, and the judge ordered compliance by the jail staff.

"Several hours of turmoil expended, I returned to the jail and discovered that the young man had given a statement upon the promise of a county lawyer and the police that the state would not seek the death penalty if he cooperated."

Chapter 9

THE BODY

Well before collaring Wilson and Olausen, the Reno Police Department had asked the Washoe County Sheriff to send a team to Dog Valley to search for Jimmy. Chief Parker went there shortly after seven in the morning to check on the start of the operation. Sheriff's deputies and Reno police cooperated in that effort, and the sheriff's department put a communications van into service as a command post in Verdi. By early morning there were patrol vehicles, motorcycles, helicopters, and officers on foot and horseback searching for Jimmy Hoff—every "man jack" holding out hope to find a live body.

RPD Officer Dave Miner, a private pilot, rented a small plane for an aerial search of the valley's pine- and cottonwood-covered areas. Miner was the only officer from the Vice Squad who had not been part of Jimmy's backup team. What he thought of his fellow officers' failure is yet unexplained. But he was there when it no longer counted. The search, slow and methodical, went on. As word spread, the search party grew.

As the effort progressed in the afternoon, a sheriff's deputy on horseback noticed tire marks and matted grass near a pond in the Crystal Peak area. Divers arrived and searched the pond's bottom. Detective Penegor, the sleeves of his white shirt rolled up to the elbows but his necktie still knotted, watched from the edge of the pond, a handheld radio in his hand. Other searchers followed Dog Valley Road and probed the brush and grass alongside the gravel road.

In the late afternoon, the searchers got help from Steve Olausen who was still at RPD headquarters. His statement was relayed by radio to the searchers in Verdi as soon as he made it. Minutes counted. Lane, Penegor and Teglia immediately got out the word as they heard it.

"He was on a dirt road outside of town by a culvert pipe," Olausen said. "They knew what side, the upslope side."

The search had been in progress for nine or ten hours when the information was relayed from RPD headquarters. RPD Officer Eric Soderblom, one of the searchers, spotted something less than an hour after Olausen talked. Soderblom had been assigned to check a section of Old Dog Valley Road from an area called Summit I southward to a point on the Truckee River about three miles away. His team had moved about a mile from Summit I and he was walking through brush and trees south of the road when he reported:

"In checking the road, we also checked drain culverts which passed under the road. In a particular drain culvert, approximately one mile below Summit I, we discovered a pile of rocks in which was a shoe."

The dirt road ran west by northwest where he made the discovery on the upslope side. The nearest tree stood twenty-seven feet from the shoe in the rock pile. Fresh tire tracks cut the dirt about fifteen feet from the rocks.

The shoe was visible from the road. "I had several officers with me," he continued. "We went to the side of the shoe. I tugged on that shoe. It wouldn't yield from the pile of rocks. I took five rocks from the pile in the area of the shoe and encountered a second shoe that appeared to be a mate of the first. I tugged on the second shoe. It too would not yield from the pile of rocks."

Crime technician Holmes helped remove the rocks to see what they concealed. In testimony later, he said he saw the shoes and helped to uncover Jimmy's body, which was lying on its left side.

"He was wrapped in a white sheet…buried under all the rocks," Holmes said. "Immediately after unwrapping him, we found four knife wounds in his chest. We also found one knife wound on each side, and another one in the back and what appeared to be a large laceration on the lower jaw which appeared to have been done by a knife."

Word of Soderblom's discovery was picked up by radio at the Crystal Peak pond, and when the searchers were told to go home it was apparent that the body was that of James. D. Hoff. The searchers registered shock. Some bowed their heads and some cried. All they could do was return to the command post, go back to their duty posts, or head home or to the nearby bar. The news spread far and fast. Years later an anonymous writer posted the following letter to Jimmy on the Officer Down Memorial Page:

I was six years old and on a family vacation in Washington D.C. the weekend you died. Somehow, someone from RPD tracked my Dad down at the hotel we were staying at to tell him you had died. It was the first time I saw my Dad cry. He called you his partner and said that you were a good man.
Signed: Anonymous, February 1, 2010.

After Olausen and Lane made the bargain, they got into police cars, Olausen with a team of officers and Lane in the second car with a lieutenant from RPD. The two cars headed for Dog Valley. While en route, Soderblom's team located Jimmy's body. They radioed news of their discovery to headquarters and to Lane, the suggestion being that Olausen's tip was without significance.

Olausen remembered it differently. "We were there as they were making the discovery," he said. "They had all converged on the same spot. As soon as we got to that area they were blocking off the spot. I didn't leave the car. Mills went to look at the site itself.

"Then some of the cops came and stuck guns in my face and said we're going to kill you. Their rage was obvious. Mills came back and ran them off. He got in the car, and it made a U-turn and we came back to town."

Olausen, as he saw it, had lived up to his part of the bargain. He had made his statement and he believed his information proved to be valuable. Lane saw it that way too. He went back to the burial site and witnessed removal of the body.

The official identification of the body was made by Lieutenant Nevada Wise, who gave "friend" as his relationship to Jimmy. Detective Captain Ken Pulver contacted Jimmy's mother, Lucille George, then living in Las Vegas, to make the official notification. Jimmy Hoff's makeshift grave was quickly closed to the press and the public.

Olausen was taken back to Reno. He and Wilson were booked on charges of murder, kidnapping and robbery. Justice of the Peace William Beemer fixed Olausen's bail at half-a-million dollars but declined to set any bail for Wilson. Olausen stayed at the City Jail at the police station, while Wilson was kept in the County Jail in the courthouse at South Virginia and Court Streets.

"I was in shock, at a point where I just wanted to die, so scared," Olausen said of his first night in the jail. "I didn't even know anybody that had been in jail."

He said he was placed in a cell "in solitary by myself"—and the officers who threw him in there pounded him in the solar plexus a few times and "tweaked" his arms. "I think I was unconscious part of the time." The cops told John Olausen that his son was in "protective custody" so that no one, enraged officer or inmate, could harm him.

Olausen said an inmate from Australia complained and asked the officers to "leave the kid alone." In response "they pulled him out and beat him up too."

The next day, at the suggestion of John Olausen and with his signed waiver as Steve's parent, Olausen submitted to a polygraph examination at police headquarters. Both his father, John, and his mother, Nancy Monnot, were there to witness the proceeding. Mrs. Monnot was dazed and hardly able to comprehend what was happening.

"We were at home in Red Bluff (California, thirty miles from Chico), and my daughter Suzanne was in the kitchen when she saw it on TV," Mrs. Monnot said. "We didn't understand it all, and we had to wait twenty minutes for the second time around. Then we saw it again."

She and Suzanne traveled to Reno, and the next day she saw her son handcuffed to a chair.

"We weren't really able to talk to him," she said. "He was doing a polygraph then, and after he passed it they said they never gave it."

"I took a polygraph test, and they were real mad at me," Olausen said. "I was passing it. I said I didn't stab him and things like that."

The polygraph examinations were taped, but it was alleged later that some twenty-three minutes of the sessions were erased. It was contended that the deleted sections contained exculpatory material, but the State answered that all that was lost were periods of Steve's crying jags.

After speeding to Reno from Chico, the detectives had apprised him of the trouble his son was in. Next, as Olausen remembered it, they promised the senior Olausen that if his son would submit to the polygraph, they would give the Olausens the results. The investigators went so far as to enter into a stipulation on the advice of Lane that the results could be used as evidence to help Olausen, which is why he agreed. Regrettably, there was neither hope nor help for the teenager.

Chapter 10

THE FUGITIVES

While Wilson and Olausen remained at large for only a few hours after burying Jimmy, the other two boys escaped with no small amount of cunning. As the morning sky turned orange, they walked to the Stites family home in one of Reno's shabbiest neighborhoods. The Stites family lived in a complex known as the Montello Apartments at 810 Montello. It was in a part of town known for its economic privation. The building was perhaps fifty years old with a pus brown-and-yellow tarpaper exterior. Broken toys and car parts littered the packed dirt yard. If grass had ever grown in the bone-dry dirt, it had given up the ghost long ago.

The complex, regarded at the RPD as a refuge for people going into "the last chapter of what's-the-use," attracted only the poorest of poor whites and equally destitute non-whites. It was the last stop before life on the riverbank in a cardboard hovel. For the RPD it was common practice at the time to send two police units on every call to the Montello Apartments.

Fred Stites talked to his brother Harley, fifteen months his senior and his childhood hunting, fishing and football partner. He needed his help to get out of town. They needed a car but did not want to draw attention to themselves.

Here, in the Stites apartment, the two killers slept after their taxing night on the Truckee. They plopped down on the floor after asking Harley Stites to go out and buy them a car. To show their seriousness, they handed him five one-hundred-dollar bills. They'd witnessed a "big-time crime," they said, and they thought it best to make themselves scarce.

Sometimes misfortune seems to operate as an evil persona from a Hollywood horror show, shooting steely tentacles from a subterranean vortex to draw more and more people into bad situations. It started with Wilson whose misfortune spawned an evil scheme to get rich quick. He roped in Olausen and Anne Marie, which led to Jimmy Hoff. The plan to rob him set the trap that snared Stites and Lani. They, in turn, solicited Harley Stites to help them because they were in trouble. It morphed into a family obligation and an adventure. Harley Stites said, "Okay." Next came another unfortunate, one John

Arthur Dollar, Harley Stites's buddy and a young welder by trade.

Having been given his mission to get his hands on a trustworthy car without attracting attention, Harley Stites, a tall youngster with intelligent looking, deep-set eyes, dark hair, long sideburns and a wide moustache, set out to see what he could do. The five bills in his pocket, real strangers there, gave him unusual power to act. He set out with a mission and ran into his friend Dollar waiting on the sidewalk.

Dollar was hitchhiking from his eastside home to the community of Stead, ten miles northwest, to get the tennis shoes that he needed for work when he ran into Harley Stites, who he'd known for three months or so. "We met on the left-hand side of the road on the sidewalk, and we just started talking, and he was telling me he wanted to buy a car, and so I recommended a few places because I was trying to buy one myself."

The two headed for Lorton Auto Sales at 1900 East Fourth Street, in a close-by commercial section that was more depressed than the El Tavern Motel neighborhood. It too had more than its fair share of shabby motels, some with rooms to rent by the hour, complete with working girls. When Salesman Ray Kunselman got to work that morning, Harley Stites and John Dollar were waiting for him. He recognized

Dollar immediately. He'd already started negotiating to sell him a used car.

Harley Stites and Dollar didn't waste much time. They told Ray they wanted a car that was ready to go and in good enough shape for a trip to Las Vegas.

Dollar sensed urgency from Harley Stites. "As we walked," he explained later, "he filled me in that his brother and another young man had witnessed a murder, and that they wanted to leave town as soon as possible." The plan was for Harley to buy a car and drive his brother and Lani to Las Vegas.

Ray pointed them to a 1972 Chevrolet Vega hatchback priced at eleven hundred ninety-nine dollars. The two made a quick test drive in the little car, described by him as "brown in color," and paid a down of three hundred fifty dollars and change. They forked over four one-hundred dollar bills from the wad of five that Fred Stites had put in his brother's hands for the purchase.

At that point, Dollar's idea was that Harley Stites would drive the car to the Montello Street Apartments, inform Stites and Lani they'd gotten the vehicle, then drive Dollar on to Stead. That was not to be. When the two got back to the apartment Fred Stites and David Lani, whom Dollar had never met, were awake and ready to roll.

Dollar recalled that his lanky friend Harley Stites had him wait outside, but the two brothers and Lani later invited him in and told him he was "welcome to go" with them.

"They were up and ready to go right there and I had my own money with me, so I didn't know how much they had or anything like that. I had my own money, and I decided, well, I had never seen Vegas, so that is when I went."

The four got in the brown Vega and headed south on U.S. 395 toward Carson City, some thirty miles away. They'd traveled about twenty miles and were crossing a wide flat area known as Washoe Valley when Dollar asked what was going on.

"Well," he recalled, "they told me they had witnessed a murder and how it happened, and then they got into details of it, and David slipped and said that he had stabbed the guy. And then there was a silence, and then we didn't talk much until the other side of Carson City."

"Then...Harley brought it up again...trying to get out of them just exactly what went down. Then they told us everything, the whole story."

Despite the criminal implications, of which they were only vaguely aware, Harley Stites and John Dollar stayed with Stites and Lani. It did not register that they were putting themselves in the position of accessories after the fact to murder and of aiding and abetting the escape of fugitives.

The route from Reno to Las Vegas covers about 485 miles of mostly unbroken desert. The route begins in high cool desert, parts of which are nearly mile-high, but in the south where Las Vegas lies, it is lower and drier. It's blistering hot in the summer and dry and cool in the winter. Between Reno and Las Vegas there is the not-so-bustling mining town of Tonopah, a few brothels and little else.

There was no lack of anxiety on the part of the two fugitives as they traversed the driest state in the United States. It is also the most mountainous and least populated state in the continental U.S. It took a full day to make the drive. The trip was entirely uneventful and the four arrived safely in the southern gambling Mecca. After grabbing burgers and cokes at a Wendy's and then buying some new clothes for David Lani and Fred Stites, they went to the bus station where Harley Stites bought a pair of bus tickets to Oklahoma. According to Dollar, there had been some discussion as to which states the two fugitives could run to, but they "settled on Oklahoma because they had lived there before." Fred Stites had friends and relatives in and around the town of Pryor, about forty miles northeast of Tulsa in the state's northeast corner. At this point, neither Fred Stites nor

David Lani seemed concerned that they were the subject of a nationwide manhunt for two deadly cop killers. It was the most attention that they would ever attract.

With the tickets in hand, the four searched for a motel for the night. That took some time, but ultimately they found one that seemed okay and Dollar rented a room in his name alone. Before retiring, they went to Circus Circus to eat, and changed eight hundred dollars at the casino's cashier and change booths, with Dollar and Haley each handling four of the bills while the other two stayed out of sight.

Dollar was not allowed to change one of the hundreds. "...They asked me if I was 21 because I had to be 21 to cash the money there, and I said no," Dollar said. "So, they didn't let me cash it. Harley cashed in five hundred dollars and I cashed in three hundred dollars."

The four changed another five hundred dollars in other places, and then they had a computer photo taken of themselves as a group.

Ironically, "It was one of the wanted poster type things," Dollar explained. "They had these listings and we picked one that was for harassing cocktail waitresses or the waitresses."

So much for Dollar's description of the adventure that would make him a felon. The next morning, he and Harley Stites drove Fred Stites and David Lani to the bus station and headed out of town.

"We started out of town, and I said, 'How much money did they give you to get back on?'" Dollar reported. "[Harley] says 'a hundred dollars,' and then we still had a hundred dollars from the five hundred dollars for the car. I said, 'Are they both in hundred-dollar bills?' He said, 'Yes.' I said, 'Well, we better cash them now.' So, we went over to this other casino."

The brown Vega ate up the 485 miles of brush, rocks and sand on the return trip from Vegas to Reno. By the end of that Tuesday, Dollar and Harley Stites were back in the Stites apartment on Montello, much sobered, and telling the Stites family of their predicament. Dollar also told his father that he was in a lot of trouble.

"He thought maybe I was floating in the river somewhere myself," Dollar said. "I asked him first if he had heard about the policeman getting killed, you know, heard it over the radio. He says, 'Yes, I have.'"

As Dollar and Harley Stites had driven home, subscribers of the *Reno Evening Gazette* read of Jimmy's killing. The newspaper, quoting Captain Pulver and others, described the killing of Hoff in a narcotics "burn," the discovery of his body and the arrest of Wilson and Olausen. So, Dollar's father knew what had happened.

"Oh no," Dollar's father said when Dollar told him that he and Harley Stites had given the two fugitives a ride to Vegas.

Dollar and Harley Stites were sitting next to each other on the family couch. "We just basically said we were scared," Dollar recalled.

Neither made any move to contact the police, but both had realized from listening to the news that Fred Stites and David Lani had been in on the killing of an undercover police officer, not just some dope dealer. The idea of what they'd done should have scared the two young perpetrators to their livers, but because of their success in escaping from Reno they felt a sense of bravado. It kept them going. What they didn't know was that the cops already had a description of the car that Dollar had bought, both their names and their expected destination in Oklahoma. So, they definitely didn't know that their days of freedom were to quickly end with a vengeance generated only by the killing of a member of the biggest brotherhood in the civilized world.

With an urgency seldom matched by government workers anywhere, the word spread to all law enforcement officers to BE ON THE LOOKOUT

(BOLO) or ATTEMPT TO LOCATE (ATL) the two fugitives. Every highway patrolman was looking for the escape vehicle but the search was about twenty-four hours late for Lani and Stites. They were about to arrive in Oklahoma.

That same day, RPD crime technician Holmes went to the pathology lab at the Washoe County Coroner's Offices. As he watched the examining doctor explore Jimmy's body inside and out, the cops in Reno were searching furiously for Lani and Stites. They knew of the purchase of the brown Vega and suspected that it had been the implement of escape for the two.

Officer Poirier, the patrolman who'd spotted the 280ZX in the field by the Silver State Lodge, continued to work his regular beat on the midnight shift after the arrest of Wilson and Olausen. That route took him past 810 Montello Street, the Stites apartment, Unit 25-A. He paid particular attention to the location since Fred Stites had been linked to that address.

As he cruised by 25-A, Poirier kept his eyes open, looking for anything unusual, anything different that might lead to Fred Stites. He passed the apartment five times on Tuesday night and Wednesday night after the killing, not seeing anything he hadn't seen before. He noted the presence of the same two cars that hadn't moved: an old white Ford and an equally old light-colored Lincoln Continental.

But on his pass at 1:20 a.m. Thursday, seventy-two hours after Jimmy's death, he saw something different. Parked close to 25-A, between its door and the Ford and Continental, he saw another car, a dark brown '72 Chevrolet Vega. He immediately ran a registration check on the plates, Nevada No. WLW067, but the response he got was "too new to be on file." He continued driving and passed on his discovery when he got back to police headquarters.

Later that Thursday morning, officers staked out the Montello apartment and saw John Dollar and Harley Stites get into the car. They initiated a felony stop, getting cover from other units, and then turned on their overhead lights to stop the Vega. Once the car was spotted, the officers conducted a high-risk stop—a well-orchestrated, multiple-officer stop with all gun muzzles directed to center mass and all sights aimed at the "ten ring."

Once the car was stopped with Dollar and Harley Stites inside, the cops ordered them out at gunpoint and onto the ground, where they were searched and handcuffed. They were then booked as accessories to murder. Chief Parker told news reporters the two were suspected of having "aided and abetted" Fred

Stites and David Lani. Bail was set at a quarter of a million dollars each.

For the cops, the stop was extremely tense since they didn't know John Dollar and Harley Stites weren't the killers of a brother officer and were only after-the-fact accessories. It was tense for Dollar and Stites also, but not nearly as tense as it would have been if they had appreciated how much the cops wanted to kill the fugitive killers and if they had realized that the cops didn't know that they weren't the killers. To their great fortune, John Dollar and Harley Stites were very careful to follow the orders of the arresting officers. They survived the encounter and went to jail. Dollar was still wearing the shirt Fred Stites and David Lani bought him in Las Vegas.

Dollar, who was wanted on a small beef by Reno police at the time, quickly decided to be as helpful as possible to soften the blow of the new beef—two counts of being an accessory after the fact to the felonies of murder, robbery and kidnapping (one count for aiding Harley Stites's brother Fred, and another for helping Lani).

The District Attorney's office offered a deal. Dollar would have an attorney and the two counts would be combined into one if Dollar would plead guilty and give evidence fully and truthfully. He'd also be released from jail on his promise to appear at court for sentencing, and although the district attorney couldn't promise probation, the sentencing judge would be told how well Dollar cooperated and how important that cooperation had been.

It went down quickly. Dollar gave the police two statements on the Thursday that he was arrested: one in the morning and one in the late afternoon. He told them everything. Harley Stites kept quiet.

On July 10, twelve days after he was arrested, Dollar appeared before District Judge William Forman and pleaded guilty to one count of being an accessory after the fact to murder. D.D.A. Laxalt attended the proceeding for the prosecution and told the judge that Dollar's involvement in the crime was "minimal."

The youth's own attorney, David Houston, told the court Dollar had not taken any direct part in the murder and had "no desire to aid and abet." He just "happened to be in the right place at the wrong time," Houston said. Dollar, whose testimony was exceedingly valuable to the prosecution, was released on his own recognizance to await sentencing.

He had told the authorities that he and Harley Stites had dropped Fred Stites and David Lani at the bus station with the tickets they'd bought the night before for a trip to Oklahoma. Within minutes, arrest warrant information—charges of murder, kidnapping and robbery—had been transmitted to police in Pryor, Oklahoma, the pair's destination. Four Oklahoma officers went quickly to the bus station to check on buses arriving from Tulsa. They spotted the two fugitives, watched them walk quickly from the station and arrested them about one in the afternoon. Two other young men with the pair were taken into custody briefly but not charged.

When news of arrests reached Reno, D.D.A. Laxalt and two police detectives headed for the airport to fly to Oklahoma to interview Stites and Lani and start extradition proceedings. On Friday morning, court-appointed attorneys in Pryor refused to waive extradition and the boys were taken to the Mayes County District Court for arraignment on fugitive charges.

The apprehension of Stites and Lani came a day after police found most of the missing buy money the killers took from Jimmy. Chief Parker, in a news conference that was called after the arrest in Oklahoma, said searchers located the cash in a wood pile. It was behind a shed near a pair of trailers in the West Fourth Street area where Wilson and Olausen were found sleeping.

The chief wouldn't say publicly how his officers knew where to look for the money, still in the bag bearing the word *Stash.* At the time, a statement could have operated to prejudice any later empanelled jury, since, by deduction after the fact, it had to have been one of two defendants who told authorities where to look during his interviews after the killing.

When Dollar entered his plea, the fugitives he had helped to escape from Nevada had already been arrested and were sitting in jail in Oklahoma awaiting extradition. Their past association with Dollar would cost them. A day later, Dollar repeated everything in his testimony before Washoe County's grand jury as part of his plea bargain. He told them that the two fugitives had admitted to the killing, that they thought they were killing a dope dealer and that they had planned to kill him for several hours before the buy was set up. This was enough evidence to establish that the murder was premeditated and that the murder was further designed and planned to facilitate a robbery.

Under Nevada law at the time, this made the crime first degree murder, based on premeditation, and capital murder (murder warranting the death penalty), based on the commission of a murder during the commission of a specified felony, in this case, robbery. With just this information there was enough to sentence all four of the young men to the green room. The State had enough to execute the boys without even giving weight to the fact that their victim had been one of Reno's finest.

The information from Dollar led to the capture of Stites and Lani and their return to Nevada. Arrest warrants had been issued for them Thursday afternoon, and investigators had physical descriptions and clothing descriptions—Stites in red pants and a red jacket and Lani wearing a blue shirt and a soft white cap.

Of course, cop killing has historically been regarded as especially heinous. In Reno, a remembered historical moment came in 1916 when a cop killer suffered an impromptu execution. According to the historical account, a particularly bloodthirsty felon faced with imminent arrest elected to shoot the local constable, then on patrol in downtown Reno. After the constable went down with a bullet through his heart, a crowd formed and its members quickly identified and seized the killer. The cop killer was marched to the nearby Lake Street Bridge over the Truckee River and was summarily hanged from a lamp post. His final benefit in life was a fine view of the Truckee River.

That hanging was said to have been the last in the city, although similar but state-sanctioned celebrations of good triumphing over evil continued to take place in Nevada State Prison in Carson City for many years.

Ultimately, use of the rope gave way to the civilized practice of subjecting the condemned to poisonous gas in the octagonal chamber. When Jimmy Hoff was killed, that chamber was still kept polished and ready for use at the Nevada State Prison, a maximum-security facility built of large blocks of grey stone produced by the same men who would inhabit the oldest prison in the state and known to many a convict as the "House of Misery."

Chapter 11

THE FUNERAL

Four days after Jimmy Hoff was stabbed to death, the City of Reno staged the spectacle that was his sendoff. One of the older cops said with complete conviction that "Jimmy had no enemies. You were either a friend or someone who wanted to be his friend." An armada of patrol cars and motorcycles occupied the parking lane and two eastbound lanes of the main street in front of St. John's Presbyterian Church—so many police vehicles that many of the 600 attendees had to walk a mile to find somewhere to stand in the overflowing church.

Patrol vehicles came from the Reno Police Department, the Washoe County Sheriff's Department, the Nevada Highway Patrol, Sparks P.D., Las Vegas and many other agencies. Platoons of somber officers in somber shades of blue, gray, green and black trimmed with gold or black, stood at attention. Every flag in the northwest corner of the state flew at half-mast.

The RPD honor guard took its position, and uniformed RPD officers, holding their caps over their hearts, filled more than half of one side of the church. Some wept openly. The casket was closed. "His face was so badly torn-up" one family member explained.

Outside, other uniformed officers mingled with mourners in civilian attire, those unable to get into the church because of the number of mourners. They stood in hot, sultry air under an overcast sky and strained to hear the words of the eulogist, the Reverend William L. Barrett.

"We were his friends," the minister said, adding this biblical quotation: "Greater love has no man than this; that a man lay down his life for his friends."

He went on to describe Jimmy as "a perfect man who had nothing but love in his heart and who wanted to make the world a better place." Then this: "He was killed by greedy, selfish men, who were opposed to everything Jesus stood for." No one, including his killers, could dispute these words.

Reno Mayor Barbara Bennett had proclaimed the day one of mourning for Jimmy, and all at the police station, uniformed officers and plainclothes detectives wore black bands diagonally across their gold stars. In Reno Municipal Court, in the same building as police headquarters, all calendared hearings were postponed so that employees could attend the funeral.

Jimmy's childhood friend and fellow narcotics officer, Frank Torres, barely made it from San Diego for the observance. His graduation from the management class was on Friday, but as he recalled, "They let me go Thursday night because of what happened. I flew out on Thursday afternoon."

Family members in attendance were Jimmy's mother Lucille, his sisters Patti Rowan of Las Vegas and sister Sandi Hutchinson of Woodland, California, his brother Paul Hamilton of Sacramento, his stepbrothers Dennis George of Reno, Tom George of Hawaii and Larry George of Oakhurst, New Jersey, and his aunt and uncle Jewel and Harry Rice of Sparks, Nevada.

Besides the family members and Jimmy's girlfriend Kitty, Jimmy's first wife Ruth attended. The loss of Jimmy came as "quite a shock" to all of them, Harry Rice remembered. Ruth stayed three days with Jimmy's aunt Jewel and her husband in Sparks. The family liked her and found her "outgoing" and "pretty tough" in handling Jimmy's murder.

"The loss to them (the Hoff family) was incalculable," Jimmy's stepbrother Dennis remembered. "To me it was anger and frustration."

The funeral was the first for any Reno police officer murdered in the line of duty in nearly thirty-two years. The last murder of an officer had come in late 1947 when an escaped Washington State reformatory inmate shot two detectives who had entered his hotel room to question him. David Blackwell, 18 years old when he gunned down the detectives, met death by cyanide gas a scant seventeen and a half months later.

As mourners at Jimmy's funeral scanned the pews and listened to the eulogy, a tall blonde woman approached the casket.

"Who's that?" queried one of Jimmy's female relatives.

"She's the sni--, the confidential informant," answered another.

"She's beautiful," said the first.

As they watched, the woman laid a long-stemmed rose on the casket, stared at it for a moment and returned slowly to her seat.

Torres remembered Jimmy's admirers. "As a matter of fact," he said, "some of us made the statement during his funeral: if you looked out in the audience, you saw a lot of the best friends that Jimmy knew. And you know—we kind of joked about it—all of his exes showed up wishing he was still alive."

Dennis George corroborated that. "There was a number of attractive single women who came to the funeral. It was impressive to me."

Anne Marie, after saying goodbye to Jimmy in the closed casket, left town. She never returned except, perhaps, to visit his grave.

The service lasted half an hour, and at its conclusion pallbearers carried Jimmy's flag-draped coffin to a waiting hearse. Officers outside, standing at parade rest and cued by the sound of chimes from the church, snapped to attention and raised their arms in salute as the casket was carried before them.

The pallbearers were Officer Randy Flocchini, whose wedding had been held six days earlier, Officer Dave Zeissner, Sergeant Rick Brown, Sergeant Doug Cardwell, Sergeant Dave Haneline, Sergeant Joe Marquerquiaga, all said to have been close friends of Jimmy. They removed the coffin after chimes sounded and the officers who had assembled inside snapped to attention.

Ray Vega, one of the few cops to attend several funerals of fellow officers, stood at attention as they carried Hoff away to the waiting hearse. As he saluted, it ran through his mind, "It's a goddam shame that one of the guys who got Jimmy killed is carrying that fancy coffin." It haunted him for years that justice for all would never include "Downtown

Brown" and his crew. Vega spent ten years with RPD, finally retiring early, feeling mostly disgust for the organization.

Helmeted and uniformed officers on 27 motorcycles escorted the procession, headed by the more than five dozen gleaming patrol cars, all with light bars flashing as a final salute to Jimmy.

"The line of police cars was beyond description," Dennis George said. "I mean it extended for miles." Chuck Kendricks, then a newer RPD officer who would later supervise the Narcotics Unit, elaborated that "Cars lined up for two miles."

Family cars headed the procession just behind the police escorts. Kitty rode in the family limousine with Lucille and other members of Jimmy's immediate family, and Ruth was in one of the next cars. Both were terribly upset. The procession moved to the Masonic Memorial Gardens section of Mountain View Cemetery off Stoker Avenue, not far from where Jimmy was killed. At the graveside service, the flag from the coffin was presented to Jimmy's mother. A local service club donated the plot and paid for the headstone.

"It was very hard for all of us," one of Jimmy's fellow officers, Steve Keller, recalled twenty years later. "We had never been to a police officer's funeral." Another officer who served with Jimmy,

Dave Ramsey, said the funeral and the show of solidarity "affected a lot of guys' lives."

After the funeral, Torres visited the scene of his friend's murder near Idlewild Park.

"I came back from San Diego Thursday night," he said. "The next day Rob Perry took me out there to where this was, and there were trees, and we walked down.

"I looked around. It kind of drops down about eight or nine feet from the street. This was daylight. Can you imagine being down here at night? What would possess anybody to want to come down here to do the deal? You could see the colors of blood on the leaves where he was there, and they were still there.

"Rob and I talked about it. Number one, you don't do it—an uncontrolled dope deal. There was no control at all on this. The sellers were calling the shots. It would have been done in an open area, or in a parking lot, where people were coming and going.

"This was totally out of—I think that as a supervisor, the first thing that was obvious to me was that there was no safety for Jimmy at all."

Torres grieved and was incensed. He passed a professional and moral judgment on Sergeant Rick Brown. In his words: "I called Brown and told him,

'You let him down. It was your fault. It was your fault you killed Jimmy. You gave him too much rope.'"

Torres recalled that Brown rejected Eubanks' pleas to have backup move in when Jimmy was being killed or had just been killed.

"They didn't have visual or voice, the transmitter for Jimmy," Torres said. "This was shit. There was protocol."

Torres was left to speculate that because Jimmy "was on a roll," Brown felt it was safe to hang back and let Jimmy handle the arrests of Wilson and crew alone. Whatever the reason, inadequate backup cost Jimmy his life and Reno one of its best cops.

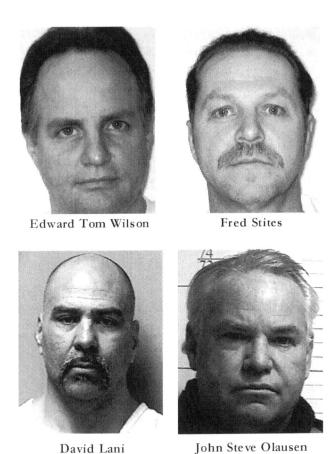

Edward Tom Wilson

Fred Stites

David Lani

John Steve Olausen

Officer James D. Hoff

BOOK TWO

NEVADA JUSTICE

Chapter 12

Squaring Off

According to the Nevada Revised Statutes:

"Murder is the unlawful killing of a human being, with malice aforethought, either express or implied.... The unlawful killing may be effected by any of the various means by which death may be occasioned."

"Murder of the first degree is murder... perpetrated by means of poison, lying in wait...or by any other kind of willful, deliberate and premeditated killing.

"A person convicted of murder of the first degree...shall be punished: By death, only if one or more aggravating circumstances are found and any mitigating circumstance or circumstances which are found do not outweigh the aggravating circumstance or circumstances; or By imprisonment in the state prison: For life without the possibility of parole; (or) For life with the possibility of parole, with eligibility for parole beginning when a minimum of 20 years has been served...."

That was the law in Nevada when Wilson and his three cohorts were indicted. They were in the deepest of trouble. Cyanide nightmares ripped through their minds, now seared by regret and fear, not euphoria and anticipation. They wanted to wind the clock back and they wanted out. First, they needed lawyers. They quickly learned that big-name lawyers don't come cheap, especially those with a knack for defending murder cases.

It was said at one time that Texas legend Percy Forman's fee in a murder case was "everything you have." The reason for that was, as he explained to his prospects, "I'll give you your life back." He also boasted that he never lost a capital case.

While Wilson and Olausen spent their first days as caged inmates in Reno, D.D.A. Laxalt, with the benefit of information from Harley Stites and John Dollar, prepared extradition papers for Fred Stites and David Lani. "It was the first I ever did. I went to Oklahoma and met Sheriff Wylie T. Backwater. Oklahoma has a lot of Stiteses."

The defendants quickly discovered that Percy Forman wasn't available when they needed him or anyone like him. In 1979, the going price for an okay murder defense started around twenty-five thousand dollars and only went one way—up. The sixteen thousand dollars that they had stolen wasn't theirs, and what was left of it had been taken back by the government.

While the Sixth Amendment to the U.S. Constitution provides for the assistance of counsel, it doesn't mean that the accused may choose any lawyer he wants at taxpayer expense. As the U.S. Supreme Court said in a 1988 case, "A defendant may not insist on representation by an attorney he cannot afford, or who for other reasons declines to represent the defendant."

As expected, the four new inmates started with Public Defenders and court-appointed lawyers to defend them from the inception of the criminal prosecution.

A historical practice of various benches in this nation, still in place in Nevada in 1979, was to help newer lawyers get started and give them small cash flows by appointing them to defend indigent criminal defendants. Presumably, passing a bar examination certified that a newcomer to the bar had the training to handle cases. But from where does expertise come? It comes from practice, either by trial and error or as an apprentice under a master. In either case, one learns by practicing on scraps. And in the world of courts, newer lawyers got indigent defendants as the scraps on which to practice.

The extradition papers having successfully been drawn up and served, Lani had been returned from Oklahoma two days earlier and Stites the day before, both under guard. An Oklahoma attorney, Carl Longmire, appeared with Lani, whom he called "one of the finest young men I've ever met." Longmire, appointed for Lani after his arrest in Oklahoma, was not a Nevada attorney and therefore not permitted to represent Lani in court. He said he accompanied Lani on his flight from Oklahoma at his own expense so that the boy would have someone with him besides the two Washoe County sheriff's deputies who had official custody of him.

The visiting attorney also said he had initiated an Oklahoma attorney general's decision to bar Reno police from the flight, but he declined to give a reason. He noted, however, that Jimmy Hoff had been a Reno Police officer. That raised, but did not answer, the question of whether he had fears of retribution or unfair investigative tactics.

Ultimately, Lani, with his family's help, was represented by Donald Kirkpatrick Pope, who had six years in law. Pope was a liberal who would go on to become a fine judge in redneck Reno's Washoe County Justice Court.

Michael R. Specchio, by his own count already a veteran of a dozen murder defenses, was appointed to defend Stites at taxpayer expense. At that time, Specchio had spent five and a half of his eight years as a lawyer in the Public Defender's Office. "[Stites] was a scared kid," Specchio remembered later. "He put his life in my hands."

Although Public Defender Atcheson had volunteered his services to Wilson on day one, the ringleader wasn't happy. Atcheson had a burgeoning case load and little time for casual conversations at the jail. Regrettably, Wilson missed an opportunity to have one of the finest trial attorneys in Nevada represent him. Atcheson, soft spoken and self-deprecating, was a genius when it came to addressing a jury. Wilson would not get the opportunity to see the master address a jury. Wilson would not even get to a jury. The machinations of Nevada justice were grinding along a circuitous and inexorable route.

Upon Atcheson's recommendation, Wilson's father, Elmer, who had traveled to Reno after his son was arrested, retained Thomas R. Brennan, considered to be "a real good attorney" by Atcheson. Brennan, a former Deputy D.A., had been in practice for five years and, as Atcheson saw it, "had a lot of suck with the cops" because he had apprenticed in the District Attorney's office.

Olausen got his appointed counsel on July 7, twelve days after he told Mills Lane and the Reno Police Department where Jimmy Hoff was buried. To his recall, James R. Forman, who had six years in law, never visited him in the city jail, and Olausen first saw his defender at his first appearance in District Court.

At that time, the Second Judicial District Court had eight sitting judges, and in a random selection process the case in chief was assigned to Peter I. Breen, a handsome man with black hair going gray around the temples. Born and raised in the stark Nevada mining town of Tonopah, and the son of a judge there, Breen had been a member of the Nevada State Bar since 1963. There were whispers about his excesses with women, especially those with "big hair," and there were those who saw him display a strong affinity for John Barleycorn.[1] Still, he had the bearing and look of the storybook judge—keen, knowledgeable and alert. He was one to move and speak slowly and deliberately, and he had a commanding presence in the courtroom, the demeanor of a supremely confident jurist, a man of fixed standards and expectations that the law as he laid it down would be obeyed. His other side was that he could be cold, aloof and quick to show anger. He

---

[1] That affinity got him a DUI in the Eighties.

had a reputation for dressing down lawyers for such offenses as not buttoning the top button of a shirt. It was rarely wise for a court lawyer to let too much confidence show in Judge Breen's court.

The four defendants made their early court appearances together, but again, it was not Mills Lane they faced at the prosecutor's table. There sat the District Attorney himself, Cal Dunlap, an aggressive 1970 bar admittee who was elected as the county's chief prosecutor in 1976. He was viewed then and twenty years later as one of the toughest litigators ever to appear in a Reno courtroom. He was known for his extreme thoroughness and love of the spotlight. It was reported that he never lost a trial while in the District Attorney's office. Some said he did not care if he convicted the wrong person as long as he convicted someone.

Although large in stature by reputation as a trial lawyer, Dunlap was a little guy. He stood about five-four and habitually wore cowboy boots. He was not a colorless, conservative guy. Before he was elected, he often wore an earring—unusual for an establishment-type in the seventies—but his friends cautioned him that such adornments might offend conservative voters. At his core, however, he was a take-no-prisoners lawyer who did not feel any obligation to Olausen despite his cooperation. Unlike Lane,

Dunlap did not see cooperation as a two-way street. In his eyes, his chief deputy criminal prosecutor had road-blocked the proper prosecution of someone who had conspired to murder one of Reno's finest by making a deal. It was a rift that would not heal.

This was a high-profile case, and it was a case the police wanted prosecuted with maximum diligence and vengeance. It was a case Dunlap wanted prosecuted to the fullest. He had known Jimmy for years, worked with him in the field and in the courtroom, and he liked him. Jimmy's death hurt profoundly and he was in a position to avenge it. Dunlap intended to look good. He had a reputation as a politician and he liked the cops. It was mutual.

As expected, Dunlap's first major move was to submit the matter to the Washoe County Grand Jury. He wasted no time presenting evidence to that panel two weeks after Jimmy was killed.

Under a 1967 Nevada law, Dunlap could have issued a formal "information" charging the four boys with murder. Such a document is based on sworn police testimony. However, when a case is initiated by way of an information, a defendant is entitled to a preliminary examination, an evidentiary hearing in court, which usually is open to the public. The District Attorney has to present enough evidence to persuade a Nevada magistrate that a felony was committed and that there is probable cause to believe that the defendant committed the felony.

Prosecutors often prefer to avoid "prelims" in high-profile cases. Defendants are entitled to have lawyers present, and that can mean delay, tactical maneuvering and education of the defense lawyers about the case. The Preliminary Hearing may also be used to educate the public. In a case where the police performed poorly, education may not be a good thing. In this case, the lost tape recording, rank incompetence and lack of evidence to support the kidnapping charge would be revealed to the public. Avoiding the preliminary hearing was the first step in a grand plan to not just deprive the defendants of a fair trial but to deprive them of a trial at all.

Grand jury proceedings are closed to all save the jurors, limited staff, and the prosecutor and, for the time they testify, the witnesses. Defense counsel, if they are already retained, are not allowed to sit through the proceedings, generally not allowed to offer evidence, and they are not allowed to otherwise help their clients or to argue. The prosecutor is in total command. Grand jury proceedings are also quicker since grand jurors respond only to the district attorney or his deputies.

Dunlap presented his case to a county grand jury on July 11, 1979, just sixteen days after the killing.

169

The panel's deliberations were short and sweet, there having been little in dispute about the central acts of the killing. Dunlap had gotten a very strong case going without wasting time or suffering any interference from defense lawyers.

The top prosecutor envisioned the green room for Wilson. Olausen could go that way also except for the shadow of the deal he cut with Mills Lane. Lani and Stites were different: very young and easily led— followers, not planners. They'd go to prison; death was unlikely. He'd argue for it anyway when the time came. Image, after all, was important.

All four of the boys had been charged with first-degree murder, robbery and kidnapping (allegedly transporting a non-dead Jimmy from Idlewild Park and possibly to California against his will and in jeopardy of his health). Kidnapping operated as an aggravating circumstance for imposition of the death penalty. Ironically and apparently unknown to the grand jurors, both Lani and Stites were long gone when Jimmy's body was carried to the car and Stites never was in the car with the body to hear the alleged "moaning."

The grand jurors, having allegedly heard testimony from twenty-seven witnesses including the six surveillance team members, homicide investigators, the doctors and assistants who handled the autopsy, and Johnny Dollar, who testified in return for leniency, indicted all four young men for murder. Lani, only 16 years old, could not escape treatment as an adult defendant in the capital murder case. Nevada law at the time specified that in a capital case the district court could retain jurisdiction to try a child as an adult instead of certifying him to juvenile court, as long as he was at least sixteen years old. In Nevada, Lani was old enough to die.

Chapter 13

COPPING OUT

As the defendants marched down the long and dark tunnel toward justice Nevada-Style, a technicality seemed to offer a shred of hope. Nevada's statutes on procedure in capital cases require that the district attorney file a notice of intent to seek the death penalty before asking the court for a trip to the gas chamber. Dunlap did not attend to that requirement as speedily as he had presented his case to the grand jury.

Public Defender Atcheson failed to see the apparent oversight as an advantage.

"Both Cal and Mills do anything to win," he said of the two prosecutors. "The idea of treachery—that's just something for the appellate attorney to worry about."

Tom Wilson, at least, did rely on the absence of the notice early in the case. Atcheson happened to be on the second floor of the old courthouse near Judge Breen's court prior to one of the hearings.

"All of a sudden all the lads were lined up, all handcuffed together in the marble hall outside Breen's court," he remembered. "You could walk up to anybody, so I walked up to Wilson, and I said, 'What are you doing here?' He said, 'We're tricking Cal Dunlap.' I said I'd be very worried about that."

"He whispered, 'They didn't file the notice of intent to seek the death penalty, and they won't be able to kill us.' I said, 'you'd better be sure about what you're doing,' and I left. The next thing I know, they had indeed entered pleas." The dim flicker at the end of the tunnel was about to go out.

Stites, Lani, Olausen and Wilson were herded into the large, ornate courtroom in which Breen presided. None had reason to doubt that Breen would issue tickets to the gas chamber.

The four paid scant heed to the head-high gray marble wainscoting on the side walls and the 18-foot-high ceiling. Nor did their attention drift to what lay beyond the three large windows facing north. They were vaguely aware that the sixteen chairs in the jury box along the north wall were empty, and they knew the five rows of theater-style spectator chairs behind them were full. Each looked briefly to see if there was anyone there he knew.

Mostly, they looked straight ahead at the five-foot-high judge's bench, a creation of dark mahogany panels with fluted posts at the corners. Behind the bench, they saw gray and royal blue walls decorated with elaborate silver tracery, all bespeaking the majesty of the law and echoing Nevada's state colors. The tracery featured two neo-classic columns supporting an arch, and in that arch the four saw the great seal of the State of Nevada, its center a raised-relief depiction of mountains and mines. American and Nevada flags, their staffs topped by gilded eagles, flanked the seal. The majestically ornate courtroom belied the crudeness of Nevada justice.

"All rise," the clerk intoned, and Breen strode through a door from his chambers into the courtroom and eased his frame into a high-backed chair behind the bench. The judge, always formal, demanded decorum, and he cast his eye across the room for gum chewing and listened for spectator whispers, offenses worthy of an instant rebuke.

The court-appointed lawyers jumped to their feet on the clerk's command.

"Be seated, please," the clerk said, and on cue from Breen, she called the case.

Each of the lawyers "made his appearance," that is, stated his name and identified his client for the record. The clerk then read the charges and each attorney, when his client was asked to plead, prodded that client to utter an audible, "Not guilty." Because of the gravity of the crimes charged, no bail was allowed.

As time went on, it became clear to Forman that there was no point in going to trial on the issue of guilt. That militated for entry of a plea in place of a trial, which all defense counsel agreed would be an inflaming experience for jurors, spectators and the news media. So, it was decided that Olausen, like his three codefendants, would also appear before the three-judge panel instead of a jury. He told his client that he'd "fry in the gas chamber if he didn't plead guilty" and that he had to enter a plea of guilty "to stay alive." Any jury, Forman told him, would sit in the court making "hangman nooses." Finally, Forman told him he would quit if he wouldn't plead.

Mindful of Forman's harsh position and still believing that he had a deal, regardless of the formalities, Olausen changed his plea to guilty to avoid a hostile jury. Mrs. Monnot also said the defense attorney believed that Olausen could serve as a sort of umbrella for his three codefendants since he had immunity from the death penalty. Olausen was made to feel he should not be so selfish as to refuse to share the benefit of his deal with the others. He would later accuse Forman of failing "to discuss and explain the nature of the charges" in the indictment and that he failed to give him advice on the legal implications of the different ways of drafting charges, particularly, "felony" murder, "premeditated" murder, and "deliberate and willful" murder and "murder committed while lying in wait." More seriously, Olausen complained that Forman failed to tell him that a state criminal code provision permitted a defendant to plead guilty to first-degree murder with a stipulation in open court, such stipulation being accepted by the court that specified a punishment of less than death.

Specchio, representing Stites, decided that a trial would do no good where there had been "a very high-profile murder" and "a cop killing, which makes it always worse." After some inquiries, a modest amount of investigation, and the obtaining of "very little discovery" from Dunlap's office, he concluded that the best he could do for Stites "was to save his life…spare him from the death penalty." Since the weight of the evidence he had examined had convinced him that a jury would surely convict his client and sentence him to death, especially in view of all the anger in the community, he decided that he would rather take his chances with a three-judge sentencing panel.

The unspoken background fact was that the judges wouldn't necessarily hear all the gory details of the crime and that they would be less influenced by emotional factors. Besides, had the case proceeded to trial, it would have taken months, which would require each attorney to work many hours without adequate pay. Unlike the public defender, the four private lawyers did not get paychecks. It would further require impugning the integrity of many local cops—the same cops that the lawyers faced day in and day out. Properly tried, even Jimmy's conduct would come under intense scrutiny. The defendants were not part of the community, essentially strangers who "would not play well in Peoria." For the lawyers, there was nothing to gain. For the defendants, in particular Wilson and Olausen, there was nothing to lose.

It was an iffy strategy. Waiving a trial and "copping" pleas of guilty to all charges reflected great risk-taking because of a central political fact in Nevada. All judges, from Justices of the Peace to Supreme Court Justices, are elected by the public at large with no screening process. More than one judge has learned that bad publicity can cost him his seat on the bench. Good publicity and an expensive advertising campaign can win such a seat. The reality is that to be a judge in Nevada, one also must be a politician—one who looks over his shoulder at the electorate in deciding any case that makes headlines. Not paying attention to politics can be and has been fatal to more than one judgeship.

The Nevada Supreme Court heard the later appeal and found that it was an acceptable strategy:

The four attorneys for the various defendants often got together to discuss the case and strategy. Due to the overwhelming evidence of guilt, the attorneys believed that it was in the best interests of their clients to plead guilty. Wilson and Olausen both contend that their pleas were not entered with effective assistance of counsel because their attorneys encouraged them to plead guilty so that they would be sentenced by a three-judge panel rather than be exposed to a jury. This advice and recommendation complained of are largely tactical decisions. We have previously held that we will not second-guess such matters when they relate to trial strategy... It is a well settled rule in this state that the standard by which a claim of ineffective assistance of counsel is to be tested is whether counsel's performance was of such low caliber as to reduce the proceedings to a sham, farce or pretense... Both counsel performed in a

*competent manner and their performance did not
reduce the proceedings to a sham, farce or pretense.*

Obviously, the affirmation of the sentences was a politically wise decision in the redneck state of Nevada where the electorate heavily favors the death penalty. Political wisdom is a requirement for all Supreme Court Justices where appointment to the Court is by popular election. Success is therefore determined by dollars raised by campaigns—dollars contributed by casinos, contractors, mines and other wealthy donors. The four indigent defendants would receive the justice that was purchased by the wealthy few from the politically wise.

Wilson was the first of the four to plead guilty. He'd pleaded not guilty at his arraignment early in the case, but Brennan had carefully explained to him why a jury trial would in all probability do him more harm than good. In reliance, he appeared before Judge Breen on October 3 to change the pleas.

Wilson, both of whose parents came from New Jersey, talked with a trace of an eastern accent. He seemed well-spoken as he admitted to Judge Breen that he had been the instigator of the events that led to the death of Jimmy Hoff. He went on to plead guilty to charges of murder, robbery with the use of a deadly weapon and kidnapping with the use of a deadly weapon. His admission was at variance with

179

his statements off the record. He had claimed he was a "gofer" for Bud, the real mastermind.

He gave clear and businesslike waivers of his Constitutional rights to a jury trial, against self-incrimination and forcing the state to prove all elements of the crime charged beyond a reasonable doubt. He also told Judge Breen he understood the elements of the crimes charged and the possible defenses to them.

He told the judge he had graduated from Maxwell High School in California in 1977 with a high B average. He said that after traveling to Reno he worked as a stocker in the Sahara and as a parking valet at the Eldorado Hotel and Casino. The judge asked why he was pleading guilty.

"Well the fact (is) that I am guilty. In a way, I feel it was self-defense."

"Why is that?" the judge inquired.

"Because I was jumped during the crime," Wilson said on the record. "I was threatened to be killed."

"Can you tell me about that?" the judge asked.

"Well, Officer Hoff, he grabbed me around the neck with a knife and kept yelling he was going to kill me."

"Then what happened?"

"I don't know, I just threw him over me and we wrestled."

"And then what?" the judge wanted to know.

"Then he was stabbed."

"…By you?"

"By three of the defendants."

"Not by you though?"

"No."

Wilson went on to admit to having smoked "a couple joints" before the killing and the judge asked if Wilson had planned on robbing Jimmy.

"Well, we didn't know really what we were going to do," Wilson said. "At first, we intended that, but, you know, I don't think it ever would have happened if Officer Hoff wouldn't have grabbed Mr. Lani."

At that point, the court recessed for lunch and the proceeding resumed at 1:05 p.m. Wilson, having had a chance to confer privately with Brennan, told the judge:

"Well, I admit to the murder and the robbery, but knowing it was a police officer, I will not."

A discussion among counsel and Judge Breen followed, and at its conclusion, Brennan conceded, "Your honor, the felony murder rule is complete. The murder has taken place during the course of a robbery, and it also makes it eligible for the death penalty." The judge then asked Wilson why he was pleading guilty.

"Because I feel I am guilty," Wilson said plainly.

Stites, present with attorney Specchio, had heard Wilson's statements, and he too pleaded guilty to the three charges. He told the judge he turned eighteen on April 6, less than three months before the killing. In response to questions, he said he had dropped out of Reno's Hug High School in the eleventh grade, that he had a C average as a student and that he had no criminal record. He also said he understood his rights and that he was not under duress to plead guilty.

Asked if he understood the meaning of premeditation, he told the judge, "To plan it out and lie in wait and kill somebody."

Stites said he was under the influence of "alcohol and marijuana" when Jimmy was killed.

"We had been drinking on and off all day," he said. "We had two beers apiece before—just before it happened, and we smoked—been smoking all day, too. We smoked two or three joints, a lot more than Wilson did. Wilson wasn't there all the time. We smoked a lot more. We smoked one just before we left."

"Were you under the influence of it?" the judge asked.

"Yes."

Stites then admitted knowing the nature and consequences of the acts constituting the crime during the planning stages and knew the acts were wrong. The judge asked again why Stites was pleading guilty.

"Because that's what was—we intended to rob him," the defendant stated. Regarding money, he said, "I didn't take none from him, but I received some."

Regarding the facts of the crime, Dunlap read the allegations contained in the indictment. Stites agreed that the charging document's words reflected what had happened. The judge made the appropriate findings that Stites acted knowingly and voluntarily in convicting himself of murder, robbery and kidnapping. Oddly, there was no canvass (a change-of-plea dialog) regarding the kidnapping. Had there been one, the court would have had to discuss Stites's absence from the crime scene when Jimmy's lifeless body was moved. He would further have had to mention the lack of evidence to demonstrate Jimmy was still alive. It was a fraud by omission on the part of the court, prosecution and defense. It raises questions still to be answered.

A week later Lani pleaded guilty to murder and robbery, but not to kidnapping, emphasizing in the process the incongruity. He appeared before Judge Breen with his attorney, Don Pope, in an afternoon proceeding also attended by Wilson and Stites. According to state's witness Dollar, Lani had admitted after the crime that Jimmy was still alive after he was placed in the car. However, given the nature and severity of the wounds, it was hardly likely that Jimmy was alive when moved. More troubling was the fact that Lani ran from the crime scene and was at the El Tavern rather than being near the almost certainly dead Jimmy.

Since Lani had at least been in the car with the shrouded Jimmy, there was some link to the purported crime of kidnapping. Stites, to the contrary, left the murder scene before Jimmy was moved, whether dead or alive. He also was absent from the burial detail. John Dollar, the judge and two lawyers convicted him of a crime he could not have committed nor had knowledge of.

Why Stites was allowed to plead guilty to kidnapping is another question yet to be answered. The Lewis Carroll craziness continued up the legal continuum into the Nevada Supreme Court. The Nevada Supreme Court did not get that answer since the Justices did not ask that question. That would have created a conundrum for the Court since there was no credible evidence to support a finding that Hoff was alive while being carried off for burial. The only evidence was the purported statements of Lani and Stites to Dollar. Since both of those defendants fled the crime scene before Jimmy was moved, the statements lacked both logical and legal merit. Apparently, neither logic nor legality influenced the Nevada Supreme Court Justices in their deliberations. It was a particularly popular decision since a cop was the victim.

It was evident in the record that the judge took extra care with the 16-year-old in a lengthy change of plea proceeding. Lani's answers to questions were crisp and intelligent, and he assured the judge he had no problem understanding the English language. He went on to say he had been born on January 30, 1963, and had a ninth-grade education. He listed his home as Santa Rosa, California.

As was the case with Wilson and Stites, Lani said he understood that all three judges on the sentencing panel would have to agree before the death penalty could be imposed. Then he was asked about his part in the crime.

"I was supposed to stab him first," Lani said. "And I did, and then I ran."

"Where did you stab him?"

"In the lower left side."

Regarding money, he said, "They told me they would give me thirty-five hundred to do it." He said the money was to come from the buy money Hoff was to bring. He also confirmed that he had no plea bargain in the case and that the District Attorney would argue for the death penalty. Asked why he was changing his plea, he said, "Because I feel that I am guilty of the charge."

The dialog then turned to drugs and alcohol, and Lani told the judge that he had not been under the influence at the time of the crime. He said he thought he had smoked two marijuana cigarettes early in the day before the after-midnight killing but did not get high.

"I didn't take any drugs or anything (when the crime went down), but we did do the crime, and I knew right from wrong," Lani said.

At the conclusion of Lani's voluntary statements, Dunlap asked him who was the aggressor at the time of the stabbing and whether Hoff provoked the attack on him.

"No sir, he didn't," Lani said. "He made no aggressive moves toward me. I made them toward him."

Lani also said he understood the loot from the robbery was to come from "a police officer," but his attorney explained later that the statement was a "slip of the tongue" because Lani did not know Jimmy was a policeman. That had been an assumption of a fact Lani did not have until later, Pope said.

As events unfolded initially, Olausen found some comfort in having made a deal with Mills Lane to cheat the gas chamber. He worried that somehow the deal would fall through—the old Murphy's Law that if something can go wrong, it will—but clung to the idea that officialdom wouldn't cheat, not even cheat a cop killer. His stifled fears were well-founded.

Olausen entered his plea on October 15, 1979. He appeared with Forman in Judge Breen's courtroom about four in the afternoon. His words, together with those of his attorney, the district attorney and the judge were preserved in a thirty-page transcript of the change-of-plea dialog, officially known as a "canvass." The proceeding ran more than an hour, and as it opened, Olausen was asked how he pleaded to Count One, felony murder. "I am guilty," he told the judge. He said simply, "Guilty," when asked for his plea to Count Two, first-degree kidnapping with the use of a deadly weapon. The kidnapping charge was, again, not supported by an admission or evidence. No surprise here, since the evidence did not exist other than from John Dollar and some interesting speculation.

Judge Breen, methodical and careful, told Olausen he would question him to ensure that he was entering his pleas "of your own free will, knowing what all your rights are." Olausen answered preliminary questions by telling the judge he was 18 years old, had finished eleventh grade, had attended junior college to finish his high school requirements and that his grades were mostly "C's."

In statements he would later repudiate, Olausen described Forman's legal services for him as "very good," said he understood the lawyer's advice to him and had no complaints about the quality of his legal representation. He would go on to rue that statement the rest of his life.

Having heard those statements, the judge then asked Olausen if he understood the rights he was giving up. The rights the judge mentioned included the right to a jury trial, the right to confront witnesses against him, the right to have the prosecution prove its case against him "beyond a reasonable doubt," the right against self-incrimination, and the right to require the State to prove that any statement he had made was voluntary.

Olausen, agreeing with Forman that the evidence against him was overwhelming, assured the judge that he was knowingly waiving those rights and that he had not been improperly pressured to change his pleas to guilty.

"I was promised a deal," the young defendant told Judge Breen. "Yes, sir. It was that I wouldn't get the gas chamber if I showed them where the body was of Mr. Jimmy."

Attorney Forman showed little enthusiasm and even less zeal in the defense of his client. He told the judge, "Your Honor, I discussed that with Mr. Olausen. The promise was made by Mr. Lane in return for information about the crime and the location of Officer Hoff's body; that promise being that the District Attorney's Office would not seek the death penalty with regard to Mr. Olausen.

"I have informed him (Olausen) that this does not mean that there is not a possibility that the three-judge panel might still see fit to impose the death penalty, but at least at this point it is our understanding that Mr. Dunlap has agreed to go along with that promise. He will not affirmatively seek the death penalty with regard to Mr. Olausen."

District Attorney Dunlap was quick to confirm the apparent deal, but with later qualifiers and actions that rendered it nugatory.

"Yes, your honor," he said. "It is true that Mr. Lane and the detectives of the Reno Police Department, primarily Mr. Lane, promised this defendant that if he located the body of Mr. Hoff or told them where it was located, that the Office of the District Attorney would not seek the death penalty. That was without consultation with me concerning that, but after researching the problem and the question, we came to the conclusion that it was possible legally, or at least preliminarily it was possible legally for us to go back on the promise.

"However, for reasons that have nothing to do with this case, primarily the credibility of the office and the Reno Police in future cases involving hostages and so on, we have, as counsel has indicated, I have made the decision to go along with the promise, even though I don't feel bound by it legally or otherwise."

The I-believe-in-the-Easter-Bunny words were lost on Olausen as Dunlap continued. "I made it clear, as counsel has indicated here, however, that even though I won't seek the death penalty and even though I would make this information available to the full three-judge panel, and even though the information was really of no use because the body was located before Mr. Olausen was able to reach the scene and show the police the location of the body, that the three-judge panel is free to do what they like in light of the aggravating and mitigating circumstances that exist, and that is a position I would also say was taken by another three-judge panel that I appeared before, that is, that they weren't bound by any such indications or promises."

Judge Breen asked Olausen what was his understanding of the negotiations with Lane and the detectives. "The maximum penalty would be life without the possibility of parole," said Olausen.

The judge next asked the teenager if he understood that the panel could impose the death penalty and that its members were not bound by promises or suggestions. Forman seemed to have understood Dunlap's treachery but choked on the words that should have come in defense of his client. Certainly, Olausen did not understand, but Forman had told him to keep quiet about any misgivings.

"Yes, I understand that now," Olausen said on the record when Judge Breen asked the question. The judge also said: "In this state, courts are not bound by promises or suggestions made by anybody." The judge then asked Olausen if he still wished to plead guilty. The lie was set up by Forman, told by Dunlap and confirmed by Breen. In Nevada, "this state," we make deals, we don't honor them

The young defendant's affirmation to the change of plea was followed by an extended dialog in which the judge emphasized that the death penalty remained possible for Olausen and then asked again, "Do you still want to go ahead with it?" Olausen was bamboozled and had just agreed to let the fraud stand. He had just agreed to unwind the deal he had made with Mills Lane. This followed the first fraud, the plea to the unsupported charge of kidnapping.

"Yes," Olausen said. When asked to provide a factual basis for his guilt, he told the judge, "I was going to be there to assist in robbing Mr. Hoff, and then everything came unglued. I hit Mr. Hoff when he had a knife underneath Wilson's jaw, and then I held the knife at his face to tell him to be quiet. I was nervous and I cut his mouth."

"Did you stab him?" Judge Breen asked.

"No, I didn't stab him."

"So, there was a plan to rob him, rob Mr. Hoff?"

"Yes," Olausen admitted, with his attorney standing silently at his side. "I was informed that he was a dealer of hard drugs like heroin and such stuff as that to kids."

"So, you were going to rob him?" The judge sought confirmation of the earlier admission.

"Yes."

"Are you guilty of the crime of murder?"

"Yes."

"Are you guilty of the crime of robbery with a deadly weapon?"

"Yes."

"Are you guilty of the crime of kidnapping in the first degree with the use of a deadly weapon?"

"Yes."

Again, the good Judge Breen omitted the necessary canvass to establish a factual basis for the kidnap charge. He had now cheated two out of three since Lani had refused to change his pleas on that count. Wilson, Olausen and Stites had each been convicted of kidnapping without an iota of evidence supporting the charge. Only the youngest had been strong enough to avoid the trap.

Next, upon the Court's invitation, attorney Forman, speaking much in the style of a prosecutor, recited a detailed chronicle of the acts his client stood accused of committing, a chronicle that was devoid of any excuse or mitigating factor.

"Does that agree with your understanding?" Judge Breen asked Olausen.

"Yes, your honor," Olausen replied, and after further dialog, the judge asked him:

"So, you still want to take the risk of going ahead with your guilty plea?"

"Yes."

After seemingly trying to open a door to mitigating evidence by asking Olausen about whether he had "taken any marijuana, any alcohol, any pills of any kind," Judge Breen inquired whether Olausen was waiving his right to be prosecuted as a juvenile. Such a prosecution would have precluded imposition of a death penalty as well as long-term incarceration. Olausen confirmed that he had discussed that issue with Forman and was waiving the right. Again, he gave up an essential right without a fight and without quid pro quo.

Even then, the system was not done sacking Olausen. After further discussion, Dunlap told Judge Breen it was possible that Olausen and his attorney could try to obtain a severance so that Olausen would not face the same three-judge sentencing panel as his codefendants. If that were to happen, he said, "I may have to withdraw any commitments that I have made to this defendant if counsel takes such a position." He turned to Forman and continued:

"It is my understanding at all times that this was going to be one sentencing with your client present, and I made it clear that if he did not plead and be sentenced with the rest of them, that I would not make the commitment that I made here in this courtroom." Ironically, Dunlap was threatening to withdraw what he had just converted into an illusory promise. He was compounding his fraud. Unlike Mills Lane, his word was not binding on him. Worse, Mills Lane's word was without value to him and he was threatening to withdraw the empty promise. Shamelessly, with the assistance of the court and the cowardice of counsel, the threat worked. Forman handed the ball to Dunlap who lobbed it across the plate for Breen to bat it into the stands.

This final transaction meant that if Olausen tried to sever his sentencing from the rest of the group, Dunlap would ask for the death penalty and would repudiate Lane's promised benefit which was already gone.

Forman responded as if his client had no bargain to begin with. "Well, I think Mr. Dunlap is not bound by anything," he said in response to the threat. "If my legal moves prompt him to change his position, then it is up to him. But my client has said that he is not relying in the least on these discussions."

That prompted Judge Breen to ask Olausen if his attorney's position would affect his desire "to maintain your guilty pleas."

"No, it has no effect," Olausen said. "I just feel that it would better my position in the case if I was tried separate."

"You mean sentenced separately?" Judge Breen asked.

"Yeah," Olausen answered. However, he would say later he still believed his bargain with Lane would stand up and that he was going through something of a required charade.

To the judge who was soon to decide Olausen's fate, it was no charade. He asked again if Olausen was "willing to face the panel...to take your chances."

"Yes, your honor, I am," Olausen answered.

The judge proceeded then to advise Olausen that a change of position by Dunlap "would mean you were facing a higher risk if the district attorney were seeking the death penalty than you would if he was not."

"Yes, I understand," the 18-year-old replied.

"Does that make a difference?" the judge asked.

"No."

"Are you sure?"

"Yes."

"Okay," Judge Breen said. He proceeded to find that Olausen had made a knowing and intelligent waiver of his rights in changing his pleas to the three charges to guilty and "that his action is taken freely and voluntarily."

The chickens were soon to come home to roost. Dunlap threw a huge monkey wrench in Olausen's bargaining machine on November 20, 1979, five weeks after Olausen had entered his plea with the bargained-for assurance that the District Attorney would not seek the death penalty against him. Dunlap filed his notice against all four defendants. Bearing the title "Notice of Intent to Seek the Death Penalty and to Present Aggravating Circumstances Pursuant to NRS 175.122 and NRS 200.033," it read:

The state intends to produce the following aggravating circumstances.

1. ...that murder was committed...in the commission of...robbery, burglary and kidnapping in the first degree.

2. That the murder was committed for the purpose of avoiding lawful arrest.

3. That the murder was committed by the defendants and each of them...for the purpose of receiving money.

4. ...upon a police officer.

5. That the murder involved depravity of mind and the mutilation of the victim."

On its face, the document stood as a complete breach of the D.A.'s promise to Olausen of no death penalty in return for help in locating Jimmy on the day of the killing. The deal made by Lane had just been officially unwound by Dunlap—unwound without even a hollow rationalization.

The notice named all four defendants. The law didn't require such notices in murder cases, but it was Dunlap's practice to file them because of a two-year-old Nevada statute. That law required that whenever a person was convicted of murder by entry of a plea of guilty, the court ordinarily had to conduct a separate penalty hearing before a panel of three district court judges, whether or not the death penalty was sought by the prosecutor.

However, the statute also provided that if the death penalty was not sought, the prosecution and the defense could stipulate to a waiver of the penalty hearing and could, but did not have to, include an agreement to have the trial judge impose the sentence. Such a two-part agreement would keep a matter out of the hands of a three-judge panel.

In Olausen's case, and his alone, that was critical. The same statute provided that in a penalty hearing before a three-judge panel, each side could present evidence of aggravating and mitigating circumstances relating to the killing, the perpetrator, the victim, or "any other matter which the court deems relevant to sentence, whether or not the evidence is ordinarily admissible."

Under the statute, a prosecutor also had the option to offer additional evidence of aggravating circumstances "other than the aggravated nature of the offense itself," pursuant to still another statute, NRS 200.033. It listed the "only circumstances by which murder of the first degree may be aggravated." They included commission of murder while engaged in a robbery or in kidnapping, whether alone or with others. The aggravating circumstances also included commission of a murder in order "to receive money or any other thing of monetary value."

The document made it clear that Dunlap was going after the death penalty for Olausen despite his rhetoric and the deal cut by Mills Lane. He'd named him in a pleading filed with the court and identifying him as a person for whom he would seek the death penalty. Despite the paper, he denied he was affirmatively seeking the death penalty. And although he blamed a secretarial error for the inclusion of Olausen's name in the Notice, he did nothing to unwind the "error"—a perhaps foxy move or more likely "just flat brazen" in one Reno attorney's words. He did not file an amended notice. He did not file any document saying Olausen was to be excluded from the words aimed at invoking the death penalty.

Forman failed to demand correction of the claimed oversight, and his client's name remained on the notice that would be read by the three judges on the sentencing panel. Apparently relying on Dunlap's casual promise to fix the error, Olausen's appointed attorney did nothing. He did not file any objection. He did not file a motion to strike the notice. He did not file a motion to require its amendment. He did not file any document indicating that Olausen was not to be included among those for whom the death penalty would be sought. He did not ask the court to sever the case of Olausen, the beneficiary of a bargain, from that of the other three defendants, who had no such bargain. This series of failures put Olausen on course to appear with the others before a three-judge sentencing panel as required by statute.

Dunlap's failure to strike the errant document was both blatantly dishonest and ruthless lawyering. The failure of Forman to move to strike was either grossly incompetent or evidence of cowardly capitulation or something worse.

Chapter 14

THE PENALTY HEARING

The penalty hearing opened on Monday the tenth of December in Judge Breen's courtroom. The death penalty required concurrence of all three judges, but a life sentence required only two of the three.

"The bottom line in this proceeding is whether these four boys are to be executed," defense attorney Specchio stated, summing up the situation succinctly in his opening statement. "I would be remiss if I were to tell you that I'm here to do anything but beg for their lives."

Against all odds, the four perpetrators stood united during the penalty phase, all attending the same hearing at which evidence of the aggravated nature of the crime would be presented to the sentencing judges. It was as though Wilson still called the shots. He was the leader of the gang; he was the oldest and presumably, the wisest of the four. He was the one who cooked up the scheme to rip off and kill a drug dealer and a pimp. He was the one who set up the deal of duplicity with Jimmy Hoff. And he was the one who gave the command to kill him while he held him to be killed. He was the one who stood to benefit by keeping himself linked to those of lesser culpability. At the same time, given the lopsided presentation of evidence and argument, he was certain to be sentenced to death.

None of the other three had any obvious advantage to gain by proceeding in the same case as Wilson. Each of the other three could have tried for a severance, and then blamed it all on Wilson. The obvious defense was that Wilson was the heavy, that youth, ignorance, intoxication or undue influence reduced culpability, was overlooked and/or ignored. No motion of severance was filed by any party. Olausen, represented by Forman, stayed with the pack that would stand before a three-judge panel—the panel that would consider the aggravating evidence and base sentences on it—a three-judge panel of hardnosed, veteran, Nevada judges who would not blink at imposing death.

The death penalty's history in the United States in the second half of the Twentieth Century affected what was to happen to the four boys. Each, by entering a plea of guilty, had convicted himself of capital murder. What remained for the State of Nevada was to decide who to kill and who to incarcerate. The state could elect death, life without parole, or life with the possibility of parole.

In 1972, the U.S. Supreme Court surveyed how various states imposed the death penalty and condemned the arbitrary and capricious sentencing patterns it found.[2] Although this effectively blocked resort by states to the death penalty for a few years, the high court did not rule that a death sentence as such was unconstitutional. Following a respite, the Court developed guidelines on how to constitutionally impose and carry out the death penalty.

Four years after the Furman v. Georgia decision, the Court issued a plurality decision saying that a state was required to structure its death penalty procedure to allow for consideration of individual characteristics of a convicted criminal and his crime.[3] The next year the Court said death could not be imposed on the basis of a probation or pre-sentence report containing information that a defendant had no chance to

---

[2] In the case of Furman v. Georgia, 408 U.S. 238 (1972)
[3] <u>Woodson v. North Carolina</u>, 42 U.S. 20 (1976)

explain or deny.[4] In elaboration a year later, the Court ruled that in considering whether to impose death, a court must be permitted to consider "as a mitigating factor, any aspect of a defendant's character or record and any of the circumstances of the offense that the defendant proffers as a basis for a sentence less than death."[5]

In reliance on such decisions, Nevada's Legislature enacted new sentencing statutes to enable the state to execute capital murderers. NRS 175.552 required that whenever "there is a finding that a defendant is guilty of murder of the first degree the court shall conduct a separate penalty hearing...(and) if the finding is made upon a plea of guilty...the separate penalty hearing must be conducted before a panel of three district judges."

That law, which took effect in 1977 along with NRS 175.554, required that the three-judge panel determine whether aggravating and mitigating circumstances existed, whether the aggravating circumstances outweighed the mitigating circumstances, and whether, based on those findings, the sentence should be death, life without parole, or life with the possibility of parole. Finally, the statute

---

[4] Gardner v. Florida, 430 U.S. 349 (1977)
[5] Lockett v. Ohio, 438 U.S. 586 (1978)

permitted death only when the panel found that mitigating circumstances did not outweigh at least one aggravating circumstance.

Viewed simply, the new laws provided for a carefully considered weighing of value judgments. The procedure and its requirements were new. There was no developed body of case law or procedural guides to tell anyone—judges, parties or lawyers— how to proceed or what factors to consider. New courses were being charted by trial and error, by guess-and-by-golly. Some factors for consideration had to be obvious, for instance, stabbing with a knife would be an aggravating factor. Others would not be obvious, for instance, determining how much significance to give to childhood trauma or past good deeds.

In this case, little to no testimony about the young perpetrators' backgrounds or redeeming qualities were ever presented in court. Even though Specchio figured that Stites would look "angelic" compared to the other three punks, as he called them, he did little to support that. Later, Stites's mother would say Specchio never asked her about her son, never asked her to testify on his behalf and never spoke with her other children about him. In her words, "I told him that I would be a witness...he didn't think I needed to be."

While Olausen's parents did take the stand on behalf of their son, Furman did not question them about the tough time he had following their divorce and his father's subsequent marriage to an unbalanced woman.

No one testified that Wilson had a life worth sparing. Wilson had said he wanted his dad to testify and Brennan and Elmer conferred in the hallway during the penalty hearing. Brennan told Elmer that Wilson would not testify and asked if he (Elmer) was ready. Elmer, years of military service and familiarity with strong authority in his background, fidgeted and asked whether he'd be put under oath and face the risk of cross-examination. Yes, Brennan said. Elmer said that in that case, he'd rather not testify. Brennan did not convince the father otherwise. Nor did he have Wilson's family members testify.

So much for character witnesses. To the defendants, it appeared that the entire process involved a giant conspiracy. To the appellate lawyers, it would appear to be a series of blunders and mishaps generated by sloth and sloppy lawyering.

At a time of uncertainty over what constituted a mitigating factor, on October 24, 1979, Chief Justice John Mowbray of the Nevada Supreme Court had named three judges to sit for the penalty hearing for Jimmy's killers. Judge Breen, who had taken the pleas of the defendants, remained on the case. Joining him were Michael E. Fondi and John F. Mendoza. All three were case-hardened old-timers.

Dunlap, in his opening, had already told the panel that he was seeking three death sentences—for Wilson, Stites and Lani. He displayed the two kitchen knives and the folding knife used in the murder and called it "the most brutal type of preplanned killing" he had ever seen. As he presented the case, the four killers "had every reason to believe" Jimmy was a policeman. He also described how, after being stabbed, Jimmy had fallen to his knees and begged not to be killed.

Dunlap refrained from asking directly for death for Olausen, but by his conduct—in light of the laws in force—he made such a penalty possible if not probable.

At the opening of the proceeding Forman had moved quickly for a ruling that the death penalty could not be imposed on Olausen because of the deal he had made with Mills Lane. Judge Breen denied the motion, telling Forman, "Although the state may not be able to seek the death penalty, that (deal) does not preclude us from considering it." By adopting that position, he rendered the deal made by Mills Lane meaningless. Was it dishonest on his part? Dishonest on the part of Dunlap? In legalese, it would be called disingenuous, a word used when lawyers don't want to call someone a liar. If the court could not enforce a good faith deal, then the court is without integrity. The only honest man was Mills Lane who was not there to argue but stood by his word when he testified later.

No doubt existed about the cause of death: stabbing with knives. The mechanism—what the knives did internally to cause death, that is, what experts call the "physiological derangement"—was another story. Whose knife caused Jimmy Hoff's death? When did he die? Was he dead when his body was moved?

These were critical questions, and the answers to such questions should have come from forensic pathologists, medicolegal investigators, and doctors, even doctors with law degrees. By virtue of training and experience, the good ones are highly skilled in the science of spotting and interpreting diseases in and injuries to human bodies. Their job is to tell judges and juries what injuries they found when they examined a body, how that injury was most probably caused and what its consequences were. In this case, the testimony would tend to link a particular wound to a particular defendant. Likewise, organ damage and blood loss would roughly indicate time of death.

In the realm of interpreting knife wounds, the way they look on an examining table in the coroner's office results from multiple factors. The obvious observations and conclusions include shape of the knife blades, the attitudes or directions of the stabbing thrusts, and movement of the blades before being pulled out of the victim. To the police in this case, the depth and width of the wounds had particular significance.

Among the implications are that a forensic investigator must usually examine and compare several wounds to come up with a good profile of the knife or knives used. Even then, experience and an ability to intuit more than mere numbers show what may be needed. Moreover, in the absence of something as definite as a broken knife tip being found in the victim's body, even the best examiner can't say with absolute certainty that a particular knife definitely caused a particular wound. Often, the best the examiner can do is to rule a knife out or say it can't be ruled out. (This does not preclude other approaches, comparing blood on a blade to that of a victim, for instance.)

Dr. Byron McGregor, Dr. Gene Llewellyn and Dr. David Berry all testified at the penalty hearing that Officer Hoff had received three serious wounds, each of which could have been fatal, as well as the lesser ones. How long a person can live and what he can do after having been stabbed—fight, run, whatever—depends on a multiplicity of factors. A significant one in this case hinged on evaluating injuries to Jimmy's arteries, veins and internal organs. The richness of blood vessels in a penetrated organ, the size of a blood vessel that's cut through, the amount of blood lost and the rapidity of that loss all help answer the questions. To a certain and unmeasurable extent, individual differences also figure in this imprecise equation.

For the killers, the issue as to how soon Jimmy died after being stabbed was critical. The obvious concern was whether Wilson and Olausen loaded a living but mortally wounded Jimmy Hoff into the 280ZX and therefore kidnapped him, or whether they had loaded a dead body, which by law is not a person that can be kidnapped, into the car. Jimmy had a partially severed aorta and a perforated lung, and it is true that the severing of a large blood vessel or an organ rich in such vessels will cause intense bleeding, followed quickly by shock and death. How quickly is a matter of situation and conjecture to a degree, a matter of some certainty in a broader sense. However, the lie was told and confirmed by the entry of guilty pleas to kidnapping. Even though the factual conclusion was unsupported by the evidence, it did not matter.

Even after expert testimony questions remained. Was one of the perpetrators goaded by the others or even his own need for a display of bravado into proving he hadn't turned chicken during the ambush? Who inflicted the three knife wounds? Did Olausen and Wilson believe they were moving a dead man?

The puzzle remains to be solved. What *was* evident to Judge Breen was the lack of either admissible or credible evidence to support the kidnapping charge. The same lack of evidence was or should have been evident to the other two.

The flouting of justice didn't stop there. Olausen had been promised that he would be spared the death penalty in return for helping police to locate what turned out to be Jimmy's body. "At the time, I made that arrangement with Mr. Olausen, there was in my mind an outside chance that Jimmy Hoff was alive and I would make that deal a thousand times over to get Jimmy Hoff back," former Chief Criminal Deputy D.A. Mills Lane testified. But after the murder, Lane resigned from the D.A.'s office and Dunlap had done all he could to scuttle the deal. That did not change in court.

He had just concluded five days of vigorously presenting evidence of the grisly crime and factors in aggravation. Mills Lane had been heard from. At that point, Dunlap told the three judges on the sentencing panel, "Now I would like to turn just for a minute to Olausen with regard to the death penalty. I have already discussed the fact that we did make a promise not to seek the death penalty. I do not want anything that I say to be interpreted as seeking the death penalty. I am not seeking the death penalty against Mr. Olausen." He then asked for death for the other three defendants—the ringleader, the sous chef and the dark-eyed 16-year-old busboy.

Mills Lane forever disagreed with Dunlap's coy manner of setting up a death penalty bid while denying he was doing so. Even in the next millennium, he said: "I told Dunlap—and this was one of the things that he and I didn't agree on—I told him we had a deal… a deal was made… we made the deal. The government made the deal."

The four defendants made individual statements to the panel of three, each asking for judicial mercy. Wilson told the judges he was sorry for his acts and that the knowledge of them would remain with him. "We all would like to have another chance," he said in a clear voice.

In contrast, Lani's voice trembled when he expressed his sorrow and begged, "Please don't give me death; it's up to you." He told the sentencing panel he didn't know Jimmy was an undercover officer and that Wilson had told him the officer was a drug dealer. "Mr. Wilson said he wanted to burn this dude. He said he (Jimmy) was not a good dealer because he sold horse (heroin) to kids."

He described how Wilson and Olausen had moved into Room Nine of the El Tavern with him and Fred Stites a week before the killing, how he first heard of the planned burn from Wilson on the Saturday before it went down, and how he told Wilson he knew of the place near the pump house where the four could rob and kill Jimmy. "Everybody knew Mr. Hoff was going to get murdered, so we didn't really talk about it," he said of the gang's activities before the killing.

Lani went on to testify how he froze the first time Jimmy walked by him on the way to the pump house, and how, as Jimmy began walking back to the 280ZX from the pump house with Wilson, "I just jumped out and stabbed him…in the back."

He also testified that he neither feared Wilson nor was forced by him into the killing. He did say, however, that Wilson told him a "wino" named Bud at the Reef had formulated the plan to burn Jimmy. "Wilson told me Bud planned it all," Lani said.

In Specchio's bid to show mitigation, he told the judges that "Fred Stites is still sick over this. He realizes the shame he has put upon his family, especially his mother. I don't think Fred Stites is a killer in the killer sense of the word." Specchio, as had Brennan for Wilson and Forman for Olausen, contended Stites acted under the domination of another.

Brennan tried to blunt the assertion that his client, Tom Wilson, was the most culpable. "If any of them had ever said no, it wouldn't have happened," he said of the killing.

All four of the defense attorneys contended in their closing arguments that Dunlap had failed to demonstrate that the factors in aggravation outweighed the factors in mitigation as to each of their clients. They pointed out the lack of credible proof that the four knew that Jimmy was a policeman and they contended no kidnap allegation could stand as a factor in aggravation. Each urged the judges to reject the death penalty for his client. Dunlap, however, had the last word.

"*Ne jamais* (never again)[6] I say to this court, *ne jamais.*" Dunlap sought to be eloquent in bidding the panel to never let the four killers to "walk among us."

---

[6] Words Dunlap had seen inscribed on the monument to Nazi holocaust victims at Dachau

Regarding mercy, Dunlap argued that the four youths had none for Jimmy, first as he fought for his life and second as he realized he was dying. Instead of showing mercy, Dunlap said, "They finished him off...loaded him up and delivered him to the mountains."

He called the murder a contract killing, with Wilson the maker of the contract and the others his hirelings, agreeing to kill for money to be used "for high living and broads and dope." He concluded that the death penalty should be imposed on Stites, Lani and "most of all for the Judas, for the Rasputin, death for Edward Wilson."

The three-judge panel retired to chambers to deliberate after hearing the evidence and arguments. They concluded their work on Friday night, December 14. Judge Breen, flanked by Judge Mendoza and Judge Fondi, re-entered the packed courtroom.

"That was the most electrifying courtroom I've ever been in, was when this panel of judges came back," Specchio recalled later. "I've never heard crying as much as I've heard in the courtroom and you could feel the electricity."

Police officers, family members and court watchers filled the room, occupying all the seats and standing in the aisles. News reporters waited, notebooks and pens poised. Judge Breen scanned the room, his face sour, sat down and read the charges and the penalties the three judges had agreed on—death for Wilson and Olausen and life without parole for Stites and Lani.

"I remember I was the first one out the door because I was so happy," Specchio said. "I was the first one out the door and the newspaper and the TV guy was there…I just said I'm the happiest s.o.b. in this courthouse and I just kept going."

Olausen wept as he realized he'd been betrayed. Rudimentary contract law provides that when there is a meeting of the minds and a tendered performance by one party (here Olausen), the other party (Dunlap through the commitment made by his chief deputy) is bound. However, the three judges on the panel and later the Nevada Supreme Court undercut this principle of law and threw the book at Olausen at bullet speed. The youth drew a death sentence on the murder count. On the kidnapping count, he received two life sentences without the possibility of parole, one for the kidnapping and one for having used a deadly weapon. On the robbery count, the panel handed him a 15-year prison term, enhanced by an additional 15 years for having used a deadly weapon. The robbery term was ordered served consecutive to, that is, after completion, of the death penalty and life terms on the murder and kidnapping count.

The knockout was the death penalty. The other multiple sentences and findings hinged on when, if ever, Olausen would be eligible for his first parole hearing. In theory, his eligibility would come about 2001—assuming reversal of the death penalty.

Wilson drew the same penalties, but he had not gone into the penalty proceeding with a no-death-for-assistance bargain. Further, his attorney had presented scant evidence in mitigation.

Lani had refused to plead guilty to the kidnapping charge, but still got life without parole even though the panel did not use kidnapping as an aggravating factor.

Stites, a youthful and immature follower, faced unavoidable life inside prison. Specchio knew the panel could have imposed the death penalty on his client. "Everybody was happy with the sentence," he said, but he added later that having the various sentences run concurrently would have been better because it would have given Stites "some light at the end of the tunnel."

Pope joined Specchio in saying he would not appeal his client's sentence, which he thought of as "a victory."

As the attorneys spoke to news reporters, Olausen, crying, and his three cohorts, red-eyed but silent, were led from the courtroom by sheriff's deputies.

Years later, Judge Breen disclosed that the "life without" sentences for Stites and Lani—that is life in prison without any possible parole, ever—were decided upon by a majority of the three judges, albeit not unanimously. The judge declined to say which of the three on the panel preferred the death penalty for the two younger killers.

On December 18, 1979, Judge Breen signed death warrants for Tom Wilson and Steve Olausen, and those warrants were filed a day later. Olausen's, parallel to Wilson's, read:

"WHEREAS, N.R.S. 175.558, 175.552, and 175.554 provide that a person convicted of Murder in the First Degree upon a plea of guilty may be punished by death where the Court determines that aggravating circumstances outweigh mitigating circumstances," Robert A. Lippold, Superintendent of Maximum Security Prisoners at Nevada State Prison, is directed to receive John Steven Olausen "for execution of the death sentence."

The warrant directed Washoe County Sheriff Robert J. Galli to deliver Olausen to the prison and ended with this: "IT IS FURTHER ORDERED, and the Court hereby appoints, the week commencing the 3rd day of March, 1986, as the time for the execution of the death penalty."

That final directive gave Wilson and Olausen more than six years to exhaust their appeals and other post-conviction remedies and then, if unsuccessful, to prepare to be killed by the state.

Chapter 15

DEATH ROW, THE FIRST APPEALS

Some of the locals voiced approval for the death sentences while others derided the softness of the Lani/Stites outcome. Some even complained because there were no longer summary executions. They yearned for the time when all four youths would have been hung from the Lake Street Bridge without a trial.

Ironically, all four received their share of twentieth century Nevada justice without a trial. While some groused and others rejoiced, Edward Thomas Wilson and John Steven Olausen suited up for travel less than two weeks after their sentencing. The two headed for death row wearing glow-in-the-daytime orange jump suits and chains—lots of chains. Their ankles were shackled together by tight, unyielding steel links, and other locked chains went around their waists. Their hands were chained to the waist chains, and another not quite long enough length of chain ran from the leg chains to the waist chains. The youths walked in pain, negotiating cold gray corridors as they duck-marched their way to a barred and heavy steel fortified bus that convicts called the "train." They were pushed, shoved, cursed and snarled at as they left the jail. Once in the bus, they found themselves chained to steel benches inside. No one is treated kindly in prison but Olausen and Wilson were showered with a special type of hate-driven abuse from both sides of the bars.

The train rumbled south on U.S. 395, a sometimes-rural highway, running from Canada to Mexico. On the way, it passed through Reno and the state's capital, Carson City. At the time, "Carson" had only about thirty thousand inhabitants, which when the state Legislature was in session, included state representatives and senators, a great many of them representing districts in the state's rough mining and cattle country. These legislators made the law, and coddling criminals had no place in the state or its law books.

It was winter and cold in northwestern Nevada. It was a time that temperatures plunged below zero and snow slipped over the Sierras from the west and blanketed Reno's Truckee Meadows, Washoe Valley to the south, then Carson Valley. The train was poorly heated and the condemned duo felt the icy chains bite their wrists and ankles as the heavy bus rolled over the thirty miles between Reno and Carson. In Carson, the prisoners, unable to see out, felt the wagon lurch and roll as it wound to the Nevada State Prison about two miles east of Nevada's Capitol Building.

The penitentiary had been built many years before near a hot spring and next to a small mountain. A pair of golden eagles nested in the dark craggy rocks high on the steep slopes and could be seen carrying rats and rabbits to their young in the spring. Inside the nearby stone walls there resided the least free in Nevada. The prison's two-story, main building constructed from gray stone blocks sat behind a thirty-foot tall guard tower—all glass on top with gun-toting officers barring unauthorized entry. Other towers kept the inmates inside. A small sign at the entrance to the employees' parking area near the entrance of the prison bore this legend: "Nevada State Prison, Established 1862."

What light there was glinted off the razor wire that lay in coils atop the 12-foot chain link surrounding the prison. Behind those coils, heavy bars covered the main building's long windows. Toward the northeast corner of the building, the gray stone blocks gave way to stucco, reflecting expansion of the ancient "slammer." A flight of steel stairs led to the roof. That part of the prison held the death row cells and the gas chamber. Gun towers stood tall in strategic locations providing fields of fire for the riflemen on duty. The only relief came from six winter-barren trees along the asphalt parking lot outside the fence. For the most part those trees couldn't be seen by inmates.

The prison was one of the oldest operating in the United States, established in 1862 when the state bought the Warm Springs Hotel and the twenty acres of land that it occupied for eighty thousand dollars. The first warden was Abraham Curry, who had sold the hotel to the state. Fifteen years later, the hotel building burned down and the present main building was erected from rock quarried at the site. The same rock was used later for several other state buildings including the capitol.

Ironically, Wilson, the compulsive gambler, arrived at the prison too late to gamble. As it happened, when gambling was legalized in Nevada in 1932, open gambling was allowed inside the prison "Bull Pen." That diversion was outlawed inside the prison in 1967. However, license plate manufacture, which started at the prison in 1928, continued for many years.

On the day they arrived at Nevada State Prison, Wilson and Olausen had forgotten the high life, money, dope and girls. They had to avoid verbal abuse, beatings and attempted rapes at the hands of bigger, older and tougher convicts. Their first order of the day was to survive the threats from within and without. Suicide was nearly as likely as inmate-on-inmate violence.

NSP inmates Wilson and Olausen clung to the tepid words of their lawyers about automatic appeals. "We have a good theory for appeal, but, of course, success can't be guaranteed." They first hoped for a reduction of their sentences to "life without." It was too early to even imagine a better outcome. They faced fifty-five years, more or less, behind the gray stone walls if they got lucky. The system which now controlled them was both political and rigid. It was no country club and there would be no joy for the two youngest inmates on death row.

NSP housed the most feared convicts in Nevada at the time. A small contingent of those men had dates with the green chamber. Wilson and Olausen joined that unhappy group. As death row inmates, they would be classified as maximum security prisoners, wear orange jump suits, live in small cells designed for one man only, and be segregated from the main prison population.

"I was the youngest person in the prison," Olausen recalled later. "You could be around a whole lot of people and be as lonely as could be."

During his first week in prison, Olausen was stabbed while lying in a bunk after getting into a conversation with "a hippie guy." He remembered his assailant as "a black guy who threatened to buttfuck me." Olausen said he responded to the threat by pulling a blanket over himself in cocoon fashion, and the assailant reached through the bars to stab him. "He was trying for my head but got my right foot along the upper arch to the ankle." It was a minor wound, the kind of thing he'd already learned shouldn't be reported. "I patched it up myself."

The attack taught Olausen, then five eleven and not fully developed physically, that he'd have to be able to defend himself day to day. He knew shaping his attitude would be the first priority. Strength training would come later. First, he had other concerns.

"Are you the guy that's going to get the fifty dollars?" he asked a new guard who was escorting him from the row to the exercise yard. "What do you mean fifty dollars?" the new hire responded.

"Yeah, you get paid fifty dollars for executing someone," Olausen explained, passing on the lore of the pen—inaccurate lore, but still, the lore of the pen.

As it happened, the executioner didn't even get a day off after doing the duty.

Wilson fared a scant amount better as a "cop killer" on the row. In conversations much later, he remembered being threatened by arresting officers and prison guards.

"It was pretty rough at first," he said. "I handled it by saying, 'Bring it on.' Then I was left alone."

Olausen was more active. He hit the prison weight rooms and buffed out.

After years as a convict, the Department of Corrections lists him as 6'1" and 269 pounds. He worked hard to survive and soon hit linebacker weight and bench pressed three hundred and eighty pounds. His massive shoulders and arms reflected thousands of hours pumping iron. It paid off. Few would provoke him, and most referred to him respectfully as "Steve-O."

"I've never lost a fight, and I've been in quite a few," he said. "Feel this." He was proud of the bulging rep-hardened biceps, delts and traps bulging beneath his denim shirt. Those muscles would make some professional linebackers envious.

That demonstration led to a recitation of the times he'd been cut, stabbed and shot.

He said he was only twenty-one when he sustained a minor stab wound in the back when he tried to stop a fight. Another incident came when he interceded for a "dorky little kid" doing time for robbing a Seven-Eleven store. Olausen had realized the kid was the target of an attack and stepped in, complaining about loud music as his excuse. One of the attackers put a sharpened piece of welding rod through Olausen's left side from the back. The wound healed without medical attention.

"If you get aid, you're telling on somebody," he said by way of explanation about never reporting fight injuries.

He also suffered a razor cut. He had been called by other inmates to intervene in a fight between a black and a Cuban. The Cuban had the advantage and the black had already been slashed. Olausen pulled the Cuban off the black, holding him in a full nelson. The black responded by socking the Cuban, who then wriggled free and slashed Olausen's hand.

Finally, a guard shot him in the butt and thighs with a shotgun when he and other white inmates went on a "rescue Mission" of "hitting bodies"—a gang of whites charging into a gang of blacks—to break up a fight among blacks. One of the group, reputedly an AIDS victim, had made a move on a young, small, white inmate and the brawl ensued. That incident, but not Olausen's lead-peppered butt, was reported.

His approach of staying aloof, not taking sides, and staying tough earned him grudging respect in the system. "It didn't come easy," he reminisced. "It had to go to the extra showdown."

On Day One as a prison inmate, Olausen found himself alone in a cell on death row and separated from Wilson. He had a back number, his prison ID number stenciled on the back of his jumpsuit. His cell measured six by eight-and-a-half feet, and his bed was a mattress of thin ticking on a steel plate. The mattress was covered with fire-retardant plastic.

"You sweat your ass off," he said of that material. "It's like a body bag stuffed with mattress filling. Now I wrap it with a blanket or towels."

Death row was comprised of two rows of about a dozen cells each. Each cell was separated from the adjacent one by a solid wall and faced a corridor on its barred side. Through the bars, the occupant saw only a masonry wall on the other side of the access corridor.

On an ordinary day, Olausen found that he and Wilson, as well as other inmates on the row, had a few hours of "walk-around time" outside their cells. Otherwise they were caged and alone except when "mixed with other lockdown guys," Olausen remembered. There also were times when, for administrative or overcrowding reasons, Olausen spent time in what was known as "old death row," a section where cells were shared. "You had contact with people, but you really couldn't trust anybody."

For what Olausen estimated was half of his time on the row, he and Wilson were in lockdown situations, that is, confined to their cells with no idea when they would walk outside again. During lockdowns, prison guards freeze all inmates in their cells, most often to control disturbances if not riots, or to search for contraband. Smuggling always has been a major enterprise in prisons. Inmates need, or believe they need, weapons, drugs and other prohibited items. Incredibly, seemingly impervious prison walls have become porous to street drugs. Many avenues have been detected, ranging from the pockets of prison personnel to body cavities of visitors.

Initially, the horrors of maximum security were not inflicted on Stites and Lani. They appeared less involved, were seen as more youthful than their cohorts, and not headed for death row. They took a different "train." They were taken instead from the Washoe County Jail in downtown Reno to the Northern Nevada Correctional Center, a medium security prison southeast of Carson City. They wore blue jeans and denim shirts instead of jump suits, and they could stroll about in the yard with other inmates. It was tough but nothing like the row.

Lani's tenure at NNCC was short. He had been there a year and a half when, on July 10, 1981, he leapt the center's wire fence and fled. He was recaptured less than three months later, on Tuesday, September 29, 1981, in Puyallup, Washington.

An extensive manhunt started when Lani escaped, and an informant's tip led Puyallup police to the neighborhood where he shared an apartment with four other young people. Police Chief Lawrence Nash said plainclothes officers were dispatched to the neighborhood and "got lucky." They had a photograph of Lani and they spotted him in a playground near the apartment. He was playing football with other youths, and the officers went to the roof of a nearby house and watched him from there for about two hours. They moved in when the game ended.

"We moved in so fast he couldn't have escaped if he wanted to," Nash said. "We waited until he finished tossing the football and was headed back to his apartment. We didn't want him to have a chance to run from us. There was no resistance because we moved in faster than he could think."

Lani had been supporting himself as a dishwasher at the Western Washington State Fair in Puyallup for about three weeks when the informant made a series of calls to authorities, giving them more and more information about him. Finally, the tipster provided the name of Lani's apartment. The informant was in Puyallup and phoned more information in as he got it.

As a result of the escape, Lani was assigned to the maximum-security prison where Olausen and Wilson remained on death row. Stites, more accepting of his fate, never tried to escape. Still, he too was ultimately sent to the maximum-security prison.

"Their excuse," he remembered, "was that they were putting all the lifers in max." While Lani lived in the general population at the maximum institution with time on the yard, Olausen and Wilson suffered on the row where they awaited an unnatural death.

The Nevada courts viewed death by lethal gas constitutional and permissible. In 1923, the Nevada Supreme Court ruled that the use of lethal gas was neither cruel nor inhumane if properly administered. The stated reason was that lethal gas could be administered painlessly. However, despite that ruling, the State Legislature decided in 1995 to substitute lethal injections for lethal gas, and the chair in the octagonal green room assumed museum status, replaced by a gurney and intravenous needle.

By the time their death sentences were imposed, Wilson and Olausen were scared. They'd become educated in what goes down behind jailhouse walls, and why. They had good reason to think day and night of death, whether by the surprise of a shank— the preferred weapon for assassination, self-defense and swagger, sharpened to a dagger-like point from whatever sticks, pencils, toothbrush handles or bits of metal prisoners have gotten their hands on—or the you-see-it-coming cyanide. They rushed to appeal.

Olausen and his family were thoroughly disgusted by the weak-kneed representation they got from Forman, who got out of the case by filing a motion for permission to withdraw. It was granted, and Judge Breen turned the case over to the Washoe County Public Defender's Office at the close of 1979.

The Olausens also wanted to sue Forman for ineffective assistance or attorney malpractice, but the family didn't have the money to hire a good civil lawyer. Olausen elected to sue Forman "in proper person," that is, as his own lawyer. His back was to the wall; he had to act quickly and resort to every possible tactic to undo the damage. He quickly enlisted the aid of other inmates, jailhouse lawyers, some quite adept at litigating. Among them was death row inmate Bernard A. Ybarra, who styled himself as "Law Clerk, Maximum Security Prison."

With such amateur help as he had, Olausen had his case going by April 10, 1980. His first legal document, or "pleading," was a motion to be permitted to proceed as a pauper to avoid ordinary court and service of process fees. That was granted, having been supported by appropriate statements of legal authority and his affidavit stating he had no cash, land, securities or other items of value.

The Clerk of the Second Judicial District Court in Reno accepted the complaint for filing the same day, assigned it Case Number 80-2962 and issued a summons. The complaint alleged that when Forman undertook to represent Olausen on the previous July 7, Olausen was "entitled to the exercise of reasonable care and skill" by Forman as "the attorney appointed to undertake and perform legal services and otherwise represent (his) legal interests."

Olausen asserted further that if Forman had done his job competently, he "could not have been convicted of first degree murder, robbery and kidnapping and would not have entered a coerced, intimidated and involuntary plea of guilty to the said criminal charges."

Olausen accurately contended that if Forman had done his job, Olausen would not have drawn the death penalty. The downside of a civil complaint, however, was that it could only ask for money damages in an amount greater than ten thousand dollars; it could not ask for a reversal of the sentence.

Forman defended the lawsuit with the aid of a civil attorney. Ultimately, however, the civil case fizzled. It did so because it was linked to the fate of the criminal appeal.

Olausen got word in the form of a letter dated January 8, 1980, from Deputy Public Defender Michael B. McDonald that Forman had filed a notice of appeal on Olausen's behalf as his last act before withdrawing from the prisoner's representation. "I have filed a motion to stay the execution pending completion of the entire appeal," McDonald added. "The stay will be granted automatically under the statutes."

He was referring to Nevada Revised Statute 176, which provided that: "The execution of a judgment of death must be stayed only under specified circumstances," which included, "When a direct appeal from the judgment of conviction and sentence is taken to the Supreme Court."

For the moment, Olausen could set aside a little of his anxiety about "the week commencing the 3rd day of March 1986." Confirmation came in an order signed by five Nevada Supreme Court justices on January 22, 1980, just six months after the killing of

Jimmy Hoff. To that day, justice had been relatively swift. From that day, it slowed to snail time.

With that appeal keeping the door open, McDonald filed two motions in the county court. Those requests for relief from Judge Breen asked for an order to permit Olausen to withdraw his guilty pleas and to set aside the judgment of conviction based on those pleas. Public Defender Atcheson filed a similar motion for Wilson. The thrust of their arguments was that the two defendants had been improperly coerced by their attorneys into entering pleas of guilty.

In contrast, the initial appeal, numbered 12346 by the Nevada Supreme Court, was against the conviction and the various sentences imposed on Olausen. Later, Wilson filed his own appeal, numbered 13267. Those appeals were consolidated and the Nevada Supreme Court ruled on them together.

From the start, McDonald was able to press the two prongs of the attack on the death sentence simultaneously. He didn't know if he should keep Olausen's appeal tied to Wilson's, however.

"At least initially," he had said in his first letter to Olausen, "your appeal will be handled jointly with the appeal of Edward Thomas Wilson. At a later time, I may decide to move to sever the two appeals. That will be a tactical decision after I have read the record."

That concern disappeared in February when Judge Breen appointed Fred Hill Atcheson to represent Wilson in his appeal. That allowed Pat Flanagan, the assistant public defender who'd been representing Wilson, to assist McDonald. Atcheson was following through on his plan to leave the defender's office.

With the two attacks moving in tandem, McDonald prepared his opening appeal brief, which after preliminary requirements were fulfilled, was filed and served in June 1981, two years after the killing. He argued (1) that Dunlap welched on his plea-bargaining deal; (2) that Olausen hadn't had effective counsel; and (3) that the factors in aggravation were improperly applied and thus improperly permitted imposition of the death sentence. A parallel appeal filed for Wilson's appeal was limited to points two and three.

McDonald contended that Olausen didn't know what he was doing when he pleaded guilty because of Forman's inept performance. This, he urged, robbed Olausen of his constitutional right to counsel. He concluded with two further points: first, because of Olausen's youth and prior clean record, the death penalty was excessive, and second, improper application of the aggravating circumstances law required modification of the sentence.

McDonald opened his written attack by excoriating Calvin R. X. Dunlap. He cited to the record for Mills Lane's bargain with Olausen and wrote, "The Washoe County District Attorney later ratified his deputy's promise... After the prosecutor's ratification, Mr. Olausen entered his pleas in substantial reliance upon the prosecutor's express promise. Subsequent proceedings in the case demonstrate that the prosecutor blatantly violated his plea bargain promise both directly and indirectly." Carefully buttressing his argument, McDonald noted that the indictment containing the charges to which Olausen pleaded guilty listed only one aggravating circumstance, yet the notice listed five.

"A criminal defendant has the right to be informed of the nature of the proceedings against him," he wrote, setting forth case authority for that rule. He added, "A death sentence imposed on a defendant without notice prior to his penalty hearing would be constitutionally infirm."

Eleven months later, Deputy District Attorney Edward B. Horn presented a carefully and well-crafted opposing brief. He avoided emotionalism, deftly orchestrated a wealth of legal theory, and argued that there never was a real commitment that bound the prosecution to what appeared to be its bargain. He also reminded the Supreme Court that under the rules, it could not alter a finding of fact and that Judge Breen already had found as a fact that Dunlap's inclusion of Olausen's name in the notice of intent had been inadvertent.

In very highfalutin legalese, Horn went on to say in so many words that Forman and Olausen, directly and indirectly, had been properly, legally and constitutionally hornswoggled, that they knew it all the time, and that they had agreed to it. In his words:

"In this case, the District Attorney, by telling the court that the promise was the product of an unauthorized agreement by a deputy in a hostage situation, was apprising the court of the circumstances under which the promise was made. As long as the promise is complied with, his approach is totally permissible. For the reasons already stated, the District Attorney complied with each and every provision of the agreement in the case."

Having dispensed with the significance of Dunlap's having presented evidence against Olausen that could warrant a death penalty while denying he was seeking the death penalty, Horn turned to the question of whether Olausen had made a bargain in which his return was nothing at all.

McDonald had urged that, "In the context of multiple defendants at a joint sentencing, the prosecutor's agreement here was in the nature of an illusory promise. His bargain gave the appearance of a significant concession of substantial value. In fact, it was meaningless."

The public defender also reminded the high court justices that Olausen, at the time he made the bargain without benefit of having his own lawyer, was an 18-year-old who had not finished high school, a youngster with no previous criminal history, and "no prior experience with criminal proceedings." In McDonald's view, to expect such a youth "to comprehend and evaluate the situation which confronted him, is to expect the impossible."

Even in this situation, Olausen thought he had a bargain to beat death, and McDonald observed that the belief was supported by the consensus of the four-defense counsel that "Steve Olausen occupied a special situation because of the prosecutor's promise—'a position of safety'—conveying the conclusion that the promise had substance and significant value to him." However, in the circumstance that the trial court permitted to prevail, Olausen was "critically deficient in understanding the consequences of his plea." On that basis, McDonald urged, the guilty pleas had to be withdrawn.

To rebut McDonald's argument and support the contention that Dunlap did his duty under the agreement not to seek the death penalty, the deputy district attorney cited to the record, particularly Judge Breen's canvass of Olausen at the change of plea hearing. Those citations included Forman's several statements that he understood what to expect from Dunlap in the penalty hearing, along with Olausen's concurrence. What the D.D.A. did not emphasize in his brief was that Olausen was a legally unsophisticated teenager and that Forman walked all too unhesitatingly and uncritically into what turned out to have been a prosecutorial trap.

McDonald, supporting his argument with references to the record, set out quotes from Dunlap in the penalty hearing that Wilson and Olausen were "two peas in a pod," that "they" developed the scheme to murder Jimmy, and that it was "they" who had committed the "horrible crime." In summarizing, McDonald wrote that Dunlap's "entire course of conduct here was an intentional breach of both the express and reasonable implicit promises given to induce the guilty pleas."

Horn urged the justices not to be impressed. His argument was simple. The plea agreement was set forth at the time Olausen entered his guilty plea. At that time, it was made clear that, while the district attorney agreed not to seek the death penalty against Olausen, the Court was not bound by this agreement and could, in light of the aggravating circumstances, impose the death penalty. Olausen and his attorney both stated on the record that their understanding of all the negotiations coincided with that of the District Attorney. Thus, according to the express terms of the plea agreement, the District attorney was properly permitted to present evidence of the aggravating circumstances of the crime which were admissible against all the defendants. Accordingly, there was no breach.

Olausen's appellate counsel, after berating Dunlap's performance, took on his fellow defense lawyer, Forman. "If Steve Olausen entered his pleas in ignorance of the worthlessness of the prosecutor's promise and its consequences, then his attorney must share responsibility for failing to fully advise his client and neglecting to notify the court of the extent of Steve Olausen's lack of information," he wrote. He cited case law to support his contention, then got to his major point, in these words:

"It was only at the start of the penalty hearing that defense counsel realized the full extent of the prosecutor's ability to use aggravating evidence against Steve Olausen. If defense counsel was so uncertain, if defense counsel was so ignorant of the trap laid by the prosecutor, then his client could not have been much better informed…Steve Olausen failed to receive the basic minimal advice…he failed to receive effective assistance of counsel."

Not true, said Horn in the prosecutor's brief. "The guilty pleas canvass makes it clear that Olausen was aware that the prosecution could present evidence of the aggravating circumstances at the penalty hearing." He went further, setting out cases decided over seven years in which the Nevada Supreme Court had ruled five times that "a defendant is denied the effective assistance of counsel only where counsel's conduct has reduced the proceedings to a sham, a farce, or a pretense."

The esoterica of the law also came under McDonald's scrutiny. He argued that Nevada's law on aggravated circumstances in murder contained an impermissible overlay of double jeopardy, this as to the robbery count. Under the felony murder rule, killing a person while committing a felony makes the killing first-degree murder, even if death was not intended, McDonald noted. That, he said, meant that when robbery was an inherent part of the premeditated murder allegation, it should not be used again as a form of sentence enhancement. Horn disagreed, urging that in entering their pleas, both Olausen and Wilson had pled guilty to first-degree murder on two theories: deliberation and premeditation, on the one hand, and kidnapping and robbery on the other. Therefore, he argued, it was permissible for the three-judge panel to use the aggravation rule for sentence enhancement.

Much more complex, however, was the defense assault on the use of the kidnapping charge for enhancement. That was because the certainty of Jimmy having been kidnapped had not been established. Kidnapping is the restraining or carrying off in some way of a person. A dead body is not a legal person. The propriety of resort to the pleas to kidnapping for enhancement, then, turned on whether Wilson and Olausen knowingly moved a wounded but alive Jimmy, or moved Jimmy's dead body.

There had been much testimony adduced and conflicting conclusions reached in the penalty hearing. There was no credible evidence that the victim was alive. This issue remained alive on appeal. There was a chance the death sentences could be reduced to life if the kidnapping charge could be set aside.

The arguments used in the motions before the lower court to set aside pleas and sentences were repeated in part in the documents filed in the Nevada Supreme Court in the Olausen and Wilson appeals.

Action at the trial court level came much more quickly.

McDonald filed his motion for Olausen on May 28, 1980, eleven months after the crime and six months after the imposition of sentence. He asked Judge Breen to set aside his client's judgment of conviction and to permit him to withdraw his pleas of guilty. The Office of the District Attorney disagreed and said so. In its brief in opposition, that office pointed out how careful Dunlap had been to dot all the I's and cross all the T's. In the prosecutor's view, little had been promised to Olausen and what little had been offered had been delivered. The sentence should stand, the office said in conclusion.

Initially, a hearing on the motions was calendared for June 19, 1980, but delay crept in. On March 13, 1981, more than twenty months after Jimmy was killed, Judge Breen issued his ruling, denying the motions and leaving the death sentence in place. In eighty-three lines of text, Judge Breen said in so many words that the proceedings were appropriately sanitized of legal defects and that Olausen got what he deserved. The prosecutor, he said, "complied with his part of the plea bargain."

The new decision by Judge Breen was appealed immediately and was consolidated with the first appeal. McDonald filed his opening brief on June 11,

1981, two years after the killing, and about three months after Judge Breen's then latest ruling.

In the appeal, McDonald challenged the imposition of the death sentence and the finding by the three-judge panel of aggravating circumstances.

Whether the Court hears oral argument is optional. The great majority of appeals are decided without argument. So, on May 10, 1983, almost four years after the killing of Jimmy Hoff, the Nevada Supreme Court's five justices, having read the briefs of the two sides, issued their opinion. They declared at the opening that: "We find no reversible error." At the end, they summed up their position this way: "Accordingly, we affirm the judgments of conviction, together with the sentences of death."

As is customary in published opinions, if not virtually mandatory, the justices set out a statement of facts on which their decision rested. Those facts were culled from the hundreds of pages of court documents known as "pleadings," transcripts of what was said in the various hearings, and the canvasses preceding acceptance by the trial court of the guilty pleas, and any other documents offered as part of the "appendix" to the appeal. These items make up the record on appeal.

The justices have attorney law clerks who go over the briefs and the record, then pass the materials on to their justices. How much to rely on clerks as opposed to doing an independent study of the record and pleading is discretionary with each justice. In fact, most outcomes are suggested by law clerks who recommend to their respective justices what outcome is warranted. Of course, the justice deciding the case must first pass the law clerk's recommendation through a political filter. In the early eighties, death for killers was very popular in redneck Nevada, especially cop killers.

The justices and their clerks cull what they want out of the record and report their version of what happened. It is not what happened but what they say happened. By the time a case is in front of an appellate court, it is the record that controls, even if that record is at variance with what happened. For that reason, a good lawyer is mindful of "making a record" at all stages of a proceeding. Justices do not revisit crime scenes or, except in very rare circumstances, take new evidence. They decide from the record.

In the case of John Steven Olausen and Edward Thomas Wilson, Calvin R. X. Dunlap, Washoe County's District Attorney, made the most of the record. Olausen, particularly, would pay a high price for that.

The summary which was only slightly inaccurate failed to address several key issues but was good enough for the Nevada high court. The crime depicted was of the worst kind, and the description painted Wilson and Olausen as essentially equally culpable co-conspirators. In the stabbing, after the first blow by Lani, the wording describing Olausen's part said simply, "The others came out of their hiding places and together stabbed Hoff an additional eight times." The aggravating circumstances were set out; no mitigating facts for Olausen or Wilson appeared in the language.

From that, what logically followed was the discussion, authored by Chief Justice Noel Manoukian, in which the justices decided to let the death penalties for Olausen and Wilson stand. They opined first that Dunlap had not breached Mills Lane's agreement not to seek the death penalty for Olausen.

As to Wilson, the justices said his plea was freely and voluntarily entered. They gave short shrift to his bid to trick the district attorney by pleading guilty before the prosecutor filed his Notice of Intent to Seek the Death Penalty. They viewed the trick as a ploy to create an issue for appeal and nothing more. In the words of the justices: "Appellant Wilson now seeks to use the precise issue that the attorneys created to contend that he did not understand the consequences of his plea because he believed that he could not be sentenced to death since he pleaded guilty prior to the filing of the Notice of Intent. This contention is without factual support."

The issue of using the pleas of guilty to kidnapping for sentence aggravation produced a more detailed analysis. The reviewing court said the issue was whether the evidence presented to the sentencing court was sufficient to establish "the aggravating circumstance of kidnapping." Turning to the U.S. Supreme Court for guidance, the justices said the appropriate measure for proving sufficiency was whether the sentencing court "could have" found the essential elements of kidnapping. Applying the "could have" test, the justices upheld the sentencing panel's finding that there was evidence Jimmy was still alive when carried from the stabbing scene. That evidence was the report that Jimmy was "moaning" and "groaning," attributed to Lani and Stites, and the idea that slits in the sheet found wrapped around his body had been caused by Jimmy's having been stabbed after being loaded in his car. Although "could have" did not mean "probably was" and certainly did not mean "proved beyond a reasonable doubt," the justices held that, "Under these circumstances, a reasonable trier of fact could have concluded beyond a reasonable doubt that the movement and confinement of Hoff increased the risk of harm to Hoff." This finding based on the double hearsay testimony from John Dollar has yet to be explained. It certainly cannot meet a simple logic standard.

The decision was a sweep for the D.A., and it left Wilson and Olausen kicking rocks on a long march to the gas chamber.

One issue, that of proportionality, was left open for later decision. McDonald had also included in his brief the theory of disproportionality. He called for a comparison of Jimmy's killing and Olausen's youth and clean prior record and other Nevada death penalty cases. Such weighting, he urged, would show it was "disproportionate" to sentence Olausen to death. In other words, he got an unusually stiff sentence for his degree of guilt. Under Nevada's legal tradition, death sentences "have been reserved for particularly aggravated circumstances," he wrote.

McDonald referred to cases in which perpetrators had multiple other felony convictions, unusual violence including attempted sodomy and murder involving torture, rape and mutilation, and previous murder convictions. He concluded that Olausen's participation in the killing of Jimmy Hoff was not so depraved that the teenager belonged in that special category of condemned criminals. He also cited a U.S.

Supreme Court case in which consumption of alcohol and marijuana had been recognized as a mitigating factor. Putting it all together, he said the sentencing panel abused its discretion by giving Olausen death and that the sentence should be vacated. Olausen was "not a habitual criminal with an extensive violent antisocial history" and does not deserve to die.

In his opposition, Horn said McDonald was trying to "downplay the aggravated nature of the crime" while Judge Breen had found it to be "'one of the most brutal and merciless murders this community has known.'" The degree of premeditation and deliberation was greater than in other cases, he said. Further, there was no evidence of marijuana or alcohol impairment, and neither Wilson nor Olausen had "a history of psychiatric disorders."

In Horn's words:

"It is respectfully submitted that the reason Edward Thomas Wilson and John Steven Olausen currently sit on death row in the Nevada State Prison is because on June 25, 1979, they carried through with a plan to murder James Hoff even after he begged for his life and for no reason except that maybe they could thereafter use the proceeds to go to Lake Tahoe to buy 'dope' and be with 'girls.' The death penalty was devised by the Nevada Legislature as the ultimate penalty for heinous, inhuman, vile, vicious and outrageous murders perpetrated by those with no hope for rehabilitation. This murder was committed by just such persons. Considering both the crimes and the defendants, the State of Nevada respectfully submits that the sentence of death in this case is not excessive and is proportionate to the penalty imposed in similar cases in this state and in other jurisdictions."

The Nevada Supreme Court heard oral arguments on the issue on Friday, May 17, 1985. Pat Flanigan, who succeeded McDonald as Olausen's attorney, argued that many crimes worse than Olausen's had not resulted in the imposition of the death penalty. Fred Atcheson, still battling for Wilson, argued that he "didn't get the fair shake we require in death penalty cases."

Justice John Mowbray commented from the bench that it seemed to him that all four of the defendants "were in the soup together" with scant difference in their relative degrees of guilt. "Something's out of kilter here," he said. Seeming to come from the other side, Justice Clifton Young found "tremendous problems" in finding other murder cases that compared to the one at hand. And Justice Charles Springer commented that drug dealers "kill each other all the time." He asked rhetorically, "Doesn't that go with the territory?"

Despite the problems apparent to Justices Springer, Mowbray and Young, the court agreed with Horn. On August 28, 1985, six years after Jimmy's murder, the high court issued its second opinion in the case and affirmed the death sentences. In a short *per curiam* opinion, the five justices ruled that, "given the high degree of premeditation in this case," the death penalty was not "wantonly or freakishly imposed." On that basis, they concluded it was not "disproportionate as to either appellant." The message buried somewhere in the murky waters of Nevada justice was that the five fine judges in Carson City were not about to undo the work of their brethren. It was "out of kilter," fraught with "problems" and a common occurrence, but neither wanton nor freaky. Good enough for government work.

Chapter 16

THE GREEN ROOM

The loss of the proportionality issue on appeal operated to terminate the stays of execution and revive the death penalty for Wilson and Olausen. The death warrants signed by Judge Breen in 1979 directed that they be executed "the week commencing the 3rd day of March 1986, and prison administrators issued a DOE, a Date of Execution notice fixing the date as Wednesday, March 12. Each defendant could be forced to breathe the deadly cyanide fumes any time that day, as long as it was at least a minute or so after Tuesday, midnight.

However, the law still allowed them another bite at the apple, this one styled as post-conviction relief, another chance in the state court system. So, it was that six years after the killing of Jimmy Hoff, Olausen still awoke each day with the gas chamber awaiting him.

Annabelle Whiting Hall, Esq., a soft-spoken, articulate and highly effective criminal defense attorney in Reno, had been named to handle the proceeding for Olausen. She was as clever as she was ruthless. She was the subject of Mills Lane's famous public comment that "I wouldn't piss on her if she was on fire." Another comment offered by one of her admirers was "Ah, that one, she's a coyote." Mrs. Hall expected to succeed, but like any good counsel she could only tell Olausen she'd do her best and keep on fighting, so long as the money rolled in.

The new counselor prepared and filed preliminary papers, including a new petition for a stay of execution, but no official word that the stay had been lifted came to Olausen. The execution date came nearer and he waited with increasing anxiety. He'd had no word from Mrs. Hall and seen no copy of a stay from the Nevada Supreme Court. Surely, he thought, she would have made the application, and he knew the rule. Was it possible that she forgot?

Inmates rapidly become jailhouse lawyers and many if not most can quote chapter and verse from the laws relating to their cases. That does not mean, however, that they understand the application of the rules or how they interrelate. That esoterica is for lawyers and judges.

But the rule Olausen had in mind was straightforward and simple. Specifically, Rule 8 of the Nevada Rules of Appellate Procedure provided in part that: "Immediately upon entry of an order of the Supreme Court staying execution of the death penalty, the clerk shall deliver copies thereof to the Governor of Nevada and to the warden of the Nevada State Prison."

Olausen had no word of that having been done, either from prison personnel or the inmate grapevine. If the stay had been granted, the prison system would know. Every time he asked he got a shrug and a "not yet." He fretted that Murphy's Law would get him again. And he thought it had.

One of his regular officers told him a day before his pending date with death that they were going to kill him the next day.

"I thought he was joking, but he said, 'No, I'm serious,' and I said, 'Fuck you.'"

Sometime after dark on a Tuesday night, a pair of guards banged on bars outside the door of his cell in C Block, which was one unit away from the death unit. The guards, strangers to him and from a prison unit other than death row, followed what was a new procedure for Olausen. He was in a cell separated from them by a barred corridor so that even when he left his cell the guards were on the other side of the bars forming the corridor, or tier.

"When they came to get me they told me to take my clothes off down to my boxers," Olausen said. A stampede of emotion swept over him and he started to resist, then gave up his death row uniform. "I was hostile, but I did, and then I had to back out of the cell with my fingers laced on top of my head. They walked me barefoot down the length of the C Block tier to a door. There I had to back up to the barred door, and reaching through the bars, they put leg restraints on and then a belly chain and handcuffs. Then they opened the door." He was young and prison-hardened but was now helpless as a kitten.

On command, he started a shuffling march through the cell house corridor.

"I was just thinking this can't be happening. This is really stupid. I'm saying, 'I've got a stay of execution,'" he reminded them again.

"Our boss sent us," the guards replied.

"Your job is killing me, motherfucker."

"I'm just doing my job."

Olausen could do little except take short steps, his legs restrained by twenty-eight inches of chain and his bare feet slapping the concrete.

"We have the papers, and everything is all set," the guards retorted as they directed him downstairs in

C Block and out a sally port into the cell house where they were to take his life.

He walked, chains clanking, through the length of the first floor of the long continuous building, then up a flight of stairs and through a pale green door into the Condemned Men's Unit. He was directed past a shower area and locked in one of the "last night" cells adjacent to the chamber. He went in the one farthest from the pale green, partly-octagonal chamber. He'd seen it before, through a window by the telephone that death row inmates were allowed to use in the witnesses' room.

"I was talking shit like 'fuck you' and so on. I was yelling I had a stay of execution and what they were doing was a mistake, that it was a murder," he said. "It was so intense. They take you up there the day before the execution. I'm saying 'I'll be back.' Can you imagine what a crazy thing that was to say?"

He was now unchained in a cell with a toilet, a sink and a steel bed frame without a mattress. He had a guard stationed outside the cell to watch his every move. "That's what they called a suicide watch," he remembered. From his cell, he could see into an adjoining room. All he could see was a man's back, a man wearing a distinctive jacket of the type frequently worn by Director of Prisons George Sumner. He knew the last night cells were used for holding condemned men for their last two or three nights before execution. Apparently, his wait in the unit would be abbreviated and it did not appear that he would be offered a last meal or a chance to confer with a chaplain. He was at the next to last stop on the last mile.

"Hey motherfucker," Olausen screamed, "you're not doing this. There's a stay."

The guards told him to sit down which made him crazier. He flared, nostrils wide, breaths coming faster and faster. He crouched wrestler-like in a corner.

"Come and get me, motherfuckers."

The guards watched him for moments that seemed interminable, and Olausen condemned the system that was finally robbing him of the last shred of hope—the hope that his bargain with Mills Lane wouldn't fail after all. He puffed up his iron pumped muscles and raged, determined to fight, but the guards stayed back. Seconds ticked by and he lost track of time. He was puffing, waiting, fuming. He'd fight from his corner.

"About 12:15 they said it was a mistake, that it was over, that the execution was off," Olausen remembered. "I was enraged. I thought it was a trick." His rage doubled. "I really got combative. I was threatening to sue."

"It's over, it's over," the guard said. "Do what you want. You want something to eat?"

Olausen wasn't buying that.

"I thought it was a trick. I thought they'd put poison in the food then kill me."

Olausen snarled and began pacing. For hours he screamed, cursed and defied his captors, raging, his voice going raspy. He stayed in the cell for perhaps ten hours, his mood swinging from sullen to snarling, his language the coarsest he could muster for any officer who came near. His very soul outraged.

About eight in the morning, two guards opened the CMU.

"Get dressed, Olausen, you have visitors," they said.

A few at NSP joke about that trip to the green room, but, officially, it was denied. The prison records would make of it a fantasy, a nightmare that occurred only in Olausen's head. Blame it on a nightmare, the system said. Maybe it was a prank. No witnesses were called. No last meal was offered. No chaplain came to counsel. Was it the ultimate prank or cruel joke? Or was it possible that it was a murder attempt that was abandoned at the last moment? Did the perpetrators lose their nerve? The director of prisons died and cannot be asked. No one else was talking, except Olausen.

"I've reflected on it, and they could have executed me. They could have gotten a freebie then claimed a mistake. You think you're going to die and you see things a lot more clearly" he said.

Meekly, Olausen put on his clothes the guards had returned, and he let them escort him to the visitors' room. There, he embraced his attorney, his mother, his sister and brother, all of them ready for a celebration. Only then did he find out that the stay had been recognized. He had survived his first execution date.

Chapter 17

FORMAN

Olausen and Wilson's loss on appeal did not extinguish their chances to survive. The next tactic in their campaign was a petition in the Washoe County District Court for post-conviction relief. The theory the lawyers advanced was that the performances of trial counsel in the 1979 penalty hearing violated the defendants' Sixth Amendment right to effective assistance of counsel.

Under Nevada's laws on criminal procedure, particularly N.R.S. 34.724, "Any person convicted of a crime and under sentence of death or imprisonment who claims that the conviction was obtained or that the sentence was imposed in violation of the Constitution of the United States or the constitution or laws of this state…may…file a post-conviction petition for a writ of habeas corpus to obtain relief from the conviction or sentence…"

On Wednesday, August 5, 1987, Judge Breen denied the petitions. "Time," he wrote in a 17-page decision, "has a way of changing everything—the good is enhanced in memory and the bad blurred. Not this bad deed. It follows like one's shadow."

The decision afforded the lawyers the right to return to the Nevada Supreme Court by way of a new appeal. It also upset Jimmy's mother, who complained, "I thought it ended with the last appeal. I've been waiting and waiting for eight years to see justice done and I still haven't. My boy has been dead eight years. I've been waiting and waiting for them to get theirs. I just hope to God I live to see it."

At the same time, the State of Nevada was building a new maximum security prison at Ely, a small mining town in the mountains along the state's eastern border. Ely State Prison was designed to replace NSP at Carson City as the prison department's maximum security prison. It featured new detention hardware, operating mechanisms and included gun posts, watchtowers and razor ribbon. The third of eight housing units—death row— opened to eighty-four condemned inmates. ESP's intended capacity in normal operations was seven hundred eighty-four prisoners and the number of personnel to operate it was three hundred forty-one.

Ely, a community of some six thousand persons made up of often unemployed miners, casino workers, business owners, school teachers, cowboys, ranchers, Native Americans, prison officers and all their attendant families, is proudly recognized as the last stop on highway 50 in Nevada. Highway 50, as it crosses Nevada, is notorious as the loneliest road in America. Truly it must be. On one end is the Reno Carson City area, the other is the Utah border. Little lies between. That which does is populated by people who drive pickup trucks with bumper stickers that say "Mining, it works for Nevada," or "If it doesn't grow it has to be mined."

The new prison, which opened for operation in the late summer of 1989 and now houses Nevada's most notorious criminals, was built with all the modern technological advances. Take down the concertina wire on the fences, add some landscaping and it could pass for a community college. As it is, the buildings are surrounded by barren spaces of crushed brown rock where not a blade of grass or sagebrush grows. The mountainsides are spectacular granite mountains dotted with junipers, pinion pines and the ancient Bristlecone pine. Some of the Bristlecones have been around since the time of Christ. The gnarly trees have weathered some of the worst weather in America. Ely is often listed in weather reports as having the lowest temperature in the continental United States on any given day.

As maximum security prisoners, all male death row inmates were transferred to Ely, including Wilson and Olausen. For them ESP was starker and more controlled than NSP at Carson City, which had a time-worn sense of human occupation about it. As in Carson, general population inmates wore denim jeans and denim shirts. Those on the row wore orange jumpsuits.

Mrs. Hall filed a formal request with the Nevada Supreme Court to be allowed to withdraw as counsel for Olausen and by an order dated November 20, 1987, her motion was granted. Except for a general reference to workload and conflicts, her basis was not made public. The Supreme Court directed Judge Breen to appoint successor counsel and he named Phillip M. Stone to represent Olausen "in all further post-conviction proceedings." Mrs. Hall was history, for the moment. Within days, Stone had sent Olausen a letter asking for a meeting at the prison.

Young and aggressive, Stone lost no time in seeing where the blame should lie. An attorney for three years with a strong chin, wide face and thick hair cascading over his forehead, he took both Attorney Forman and the Office of the District Attorney to task in a no-nonsense appeal brief. He argued that Olausen faced the death penalty unjustly because of the arrogance of the prosecutor and the incompetence of the defense counsel.

Larry Wishart, for Wilson, was even more critical, accusing the prosecutors of "blatant intellectual dishonesty" and taking a position that was "ripe with disrespect for anyone considering this case." Deputy Prosecutor Gary H. Hatlestad manifested outrage at those particular insults on behalf of the district attorney's office.

Hatlestad filed a motion asking the Supremes to strike certain portions of Stone's brief for "making disparaging remarks against opposing counsel." But it turned out to be Hatlestad who had to dine on breast of crow.

Stone, right after receiving Hatlestad's opposing brief, filed his own motion to strike the prosecutor's brief because it failed to make specific page and line number references to the record on appeal in setting forth specific facts. Specifying volume, page and line numbers in briefs gives reviewing justices ready access to the raw materials of the case. This lets them check accuracy and context on a fact-by-fact basis.

Hatlestad "fessed up" to ignoring the rules. In his opposing brief, he said he could offer "no real excuse" for not referencing his brief. He reminded the justices they made "a clear, plain and concise statement of the operative facts" in their first decision in which they denied the appeal of Wilson and Olausen. As it was, however, that statement dealt entirely with a different theory for appeal. The facts set out were those relating to the commission of the crime, not how the defense counsel performed.

Hatlestad was not discouraged. He told the justices that to redo the statement of facts would have required "another eighty page plus brief" and that, in approaching the new appeal the first time, "this writer was troubled by writing a lengthy statement when this Court had already authored a very precise one." He also disputed Stone's contention that the State's failures would prejudice Olausen.

The Court indicated no sympathy and instead was critical. The order signed by three justices said the quoted opinion was "devoid of any facts relevant to appellants' (then pending) petitions for post-conviction relief" and "provides no information relevant" to those petitions. Hatlestad was given twenty days to file a new brief containing "a proper statement of the case and facts relating to the post-conviction proceedings." The justices specifically demanded "citations to the record supporting each and every factual assertion."

The Supreme Court heard arguments from Wishart and Stone on Monday, November 14, 1988.

From the bench, Justice Clifton Young told Stone, "I agree it wasn't a model defense. Would it have made any difference?" Wishart argued that Jimmy was dead or so nearly dead when he was moved that a kidnapping wasn't possible and that, therefore, Wilson was improperly sentenced to death. Justice Tom Steffen rejected that, observing that the high court already had upheld the kidnapping convictions.

After hearing the argument, the justices retired to consider what they had heard and what they had read in Wishart's and Stone's briefs and the transcripts of the proceedings before the three-judge sentencing panel.

In their *per curiam* opinion issued on March 30, 1989, the justices vacated Olausen's death sentence and returned his case to the district court in Reno for a new sentencing hearing. The reason was a straightforward, gloves-off finding that Forman had stumbled fatally in his duty to provide a decent defense for Olausen, or in the words of the high court, "Forman's failure to present more mitigation evidence on Olausen's behalf was error serious enough to abrogate Olausen's Sixth Amendment right to counsel."

The justices disparaged Forman's performance from the start. They noted that: "Olausen's claim has merit because the record indicated that his attorney neglected to present a wealth of mitigating evidence that was available to him at the time of the penalty hearing. Moreover, counsel made several damaging remarks to the sentencing panel during his opening statement and closing argument."

The justices agreed with the arguments of Olausen's counsel that Forman's "decision not to present a large body of mitigating evidence, coupled with counsel's egregious remarks before the sentencing panel, denied him the effective assistance of counsel."

In an appropriately emotionless and dry statement of the facts of the sentencing hearing, the justices wrote that: "The bulk of the five-day penalty hearing consisted of the district attorney's presentation of aggravating factors. James Forman, Olausen's trial counsel, asked only his mother and father to testify on his behalf. Although their testimony was relevant, it would naturally appear somewhat biased in favor of Olausen. Incredibly, given the wealth of other mitigating evidence presented by Forman in support of Olausen's attempt to avoid a death sentence."

The justices also criticized Forman's refusal "to allow Olausen's parents to testify as to his difficult childhood following their divorce and Mr. Olausen's remarriage to an emotionally unstable woman." And further, "He also refused to present the father's testimony concerning phone calls made to both parents two days before the murder, when the 18-year-old Olausen asked permission to return home, but was rejected by both of his parents."

The Supreme Court did not stop there. The opinion also made a permanent record of the fact that Olausen's father testified in the 1987 post-conviction relief hearing that he told Forman in 1979 about Olausen's "difficult childhood," the family's problems and how Olausen involved himself in sports and scouting. "According to Mr. Olausen," the opinion said, "Forman's response to this information was, 'He's not a kid anymore, he's a murderer. He's someone that it would be a waste of time to present that type of background...and this stuff...it would just piss off the judge.'" Based on that, the justices opined that, "Apparently, Mr. Forman decided that an attempt to save his client from the death penalty would not be worth the effort."

The justices went further, observing that Forman "failed to take advantage" of a Nevada statute permitting court-appointed attorneys to hire investigators to help them prepare defenses for their client's defense. Compounding this omission was the attitude reflected by the justices' statement that: "When Mr. Olausen personally offered to hire an investigator in the preparation of his son's case, Forman became defensive and said: 'I'm only getting $7500 for this case. If I didn't want to handle it or I didn't think I could, I sure wouldn't bother with it.... It's not important, that type of stuff, it would just waste the court's time.'"

Adding fuel to this part of the fire, the justices noted that even before the original sentencing, Olausen's sister Suzanne contacted some twenty people in their home town of Chico, California who told her that they would testify for Olausen. However, when she told Forman, he "discouraged the idea because it would waste court time."

The justices also found that Forman had no interest in Olausen's dyslexia problem since, "It didn't have anything to do with the crime that Olausen had committed." Moreover, they wrote that when Suzanne informed Forman that Olausen had "saved his cousin's life when they were children, Forman responded: 'He was a child. They were boys. It (doesn't) have any bearing. He's a man now.'"

And as if Forman's lack of interest in showing Olausen's good side were not enough, the justices also acknowledged that Reno police detectives "interrogated Olausen for approximately one hour and ten minutes," during which time they "ostensibly recorded Olausen's entire confession." Mysteriously, however, "there were over fifteen minutes of time unaccounted for on the cassette tape." Olausen's father was present and testified later that the officers paused the tape recorder when his son "became emotional."

As seen by the justices: "Moreover, although he remembered his son expressing remorse for his crime and sympathy for the victim's family, Mr. Olausen testified that the final recording included none of these statements." The father mentioned the gaps to Forman several times, the justices said, but Forman's reply was "that since 'the whole courtroom's full of cops...(it would) be useless to try and bring something like this when we're the bad guys.'"

The justices took note of still another omitted opportunity for presenting mitigating testimony, that relating to 1979 visits of Douglas Mathewson, a Mormon bishop, to Olausen in jail. "On those occasions," the justices wrote, "Olausen expressed his sorrow and remorse for his actions. Olausen also asked the bishop for instruction in the process of repenting. Mathewson visited Forman prior to the sentencing hearing and raised the issues of Olausen's sorrow, remorse and repentance. Forman never asked Mathewson to testify."

The justices saw remorse as a key factor in averting a death sentence. They said the sentencing panel found that Stites and Lani both demonstrated remorse and neither drew the death penalty from the panel. On that basis, they disagreed with "Forman's conclusion that it would have been 'useless' to present evidence of Olausen's remorse."

Sentencing judges must have "the fullest information possible regarding the defendant's life and characteristics," the justices said. On that basis, the "gravity and sheer quantity" of Forman's omissions constituted "error serious enough to abrogate Olausen's Sixth Amendment right to counsel." In the absence of those errors, the justices said, "The sentencing panel would have concluded that the balancing of aggravating and mitigating circumstances did not warrant death."

The justices had more criticism for Forman, whose "performance before the sentencing panel was remarkable not for the forcefulness of his advocacy, but rather for the ambivalence he showed toward Olausen's case." They found that in both his opening and closing arguments he alternated between comments intended to spare his client from the death penalty, and remarks that were more appropriate for the district attorney."

The justices noted that Forman told the sentencing judges that, "I could put him up to say he is sorry, but everybody is sorry at this time. I'm sorry and I'm sure they would say they are sorry." They found that he downplayed the significance of Olausen's remorse, saying, "The remorse today is not going to bring Officer Hoff back. It isn't going to help these defendants."

"Finally," the three justices wrote in concurrence, "Forman summed up the reasons for not giving Olausen the death penalty: 'I contend that the circumstances just aren't there… The evidence of Mr. Wilson's influences over these men, I don't know. He's young; he's eighteen years of age, and he is sorry, and I think that is probably the most significant mitigating circumstance.'"

They added, "from bad to worse, in his closing argument, Forman made several comments that assisted the prosecution rather than his client. Forman warmed[7] the judges to Olausen's plea for mercy by stating: 'I don't know if Fred stuck him full of holes or if Steve (Olausen) stuck him full of holes.'

"Later, Forman championed the district attorney's position when he said, 'I certainly hope the court hasn't been offended by possibly my curt attitude with regard to Mr. Olausen, but I think this court has a duty…has a duty to law enforcement, has

---

[7] A seeming misuse of the word unless the justices intended sarcasm.

a duty to the prosecution to weigh this case from a legal standpoint.'

"Forman continued his sterling advocacy with the thought that: 'I'm sure friends of Officer Hoff…I'm sure if it was my friend, I would want them dead. But I would have to go home and have to think about the oath that I took, the education that I have spent half of my life acquiring, and the fact that this court has a duty to weigh the circumstances of this case…' We believe that after Mr. Forman made the above comments, there was little doubt as to which penalty Olausen would receive."

The decision was no clean sweep for Olausen, but it did give him a chance to get a reduced penalty. He'd escaped the gas chamber for the moment, but it did not wipe out his sentence of life without parole.

For Wilson, the decision meant little. They found that statements from Wilson's family members might not have helped. "Given counsel's legitimate concerns that Wilson's own family might deliver damaging testimony, his decision not to call the family did not vitiate Wilson's Sixth Amendment right to counsel," the justices wrote. They also noted that Wilson's counsel had elicited testimony from his client's father and brother. That was when Wilson had "worked at his father's service station as a boy in order to assist the family during difficult financial times," and that Wilson had done well in high school athletics and leadership. However, the justices found that "the limited amount of mitigating evidence offered by Wilson's father and brother...does not outweigh the aggravating circumstances."

Ultimately, the four justices who joined in the opinion agreed that Wilson had been adequately represented so his death sentence would not be lifted. That appeal was the final one available to Wilson in the Nevada court system, and it left him with recourse only to a federal court proceeding. His attorney filed a notice of intent to appeal his case in the federal court in Reno, and U.S. District Court Judge Phillip Pro of Las Vegas issued yet another stay of execution, blocking the June 13 execution ordered by Judge Breen earlier.

Again, Jimmy's mother Lucille felt she had been deprived of justice. She told news reporters, "Oh, for Christ's sake, almost ten years I've been waiting and waiting. I think it stinks. They both deserve the electric chair."

A similar complaint came from RPD Officer Eubanks, who had been on the surveillance team the night Jimmy was killed. "The rules of the game are more important than the truth," he said. "Can Jimmy Hoff appeal his sentence? No, because Jimmy Hoff got a death sentence right on the spot." An old salt not particularly fond of the detective said that "Brown and Eubanks should have been on death row not the stupid fuckin' kids." Obviously, not all the RPD sympathized with Eubanks.

Olausen's death penalty challenge had new life. He had a second chance to present factors of mitigation. It was a new case and called for a new lawyer, a privately retained lawyer. During his ten years behind bars, he made a new friend who had family money. The family paid Mrs. Hall a fee of thirty-two thousand dollars to handle the second penalty hearing. She came out as the proverbial tiger, albeit of the paper sort, filing a flurry of motions. She asked Judge Breen to strike Olausen's name from the 1979 Notice of Intent to Seek Death Penalty. She asked for an order to keep out evidence of the purported match between the bloody holes in the winding sheet and Jimmy's abdomen. Her reason was that the State had failed to preserve the mattress as evidence that Stites and Lani had used it for knife practice. She asked that Olausen's confession to Mills Lane be suppressed. That motion was based on timing of discrepancies in the tape recordings, which she called "materially inaccurate and misleading."

Not surprisingly, Judge Breen denied the motions. In Reno's legal community, some defense attorneys referred to him outside of the courtroom as

"Black Pete" and complained that his rulings tended unfairly to favor the prosecution in criminal matters. Because of the perceived bias, some competent lawyers preferred not to appear in his court. Whether he was biased or simply misled in this matter was unknown.

What is known is that in the initial penalty hearing Judge Breen permitted the hearsay evidence of the purported kidnapping to be admitted. He also permitted the sentencing panel to consider the death penalty for Olausen despite the deal made by Mills Lane. And, he accepted three guilty pleas to kidnapping without any basis.

In keeping with the order of the Supreme Court, a new three-judge sentencing panel was named, Judge Breen having removed himself from the case in May. The judges were Second District Judge Roy L. Torvinen of Reno, Fourth District Judge Joseph O. McDaniel of Elko, and Eighth District Judge Jack Lehman of Las Vegas. Judge Torvinen was an even-tempered, well-liked jurist with a dry sense of humor. He looked like he was born old and wise. Judge McDaniel was what one would expect from the cowboy country of Elko. He was definitely not the judge one would pick to reduce a death penalty in a cop killing. Judge Lehman, also known as "Screaming Jack" was a cipher. Generally seen as slightly liberal, he was unpredictable and easily angered. The three comprised the hand that was dealt and Olausen and his new lawyer had to play it. Ironically, the ex-fighter Mills Lane and Annabell Hall, the "coyote" he wouldn't "piss on" were on the same side—the side that favored Olausen.

In a hearing that began on Monday, December 4, 1989, and lasted four and a half days, Mrs. Hall put her best evidence before the judge and did her best to minimize the impact of the unfavorable. Family, friends and fellow Mormons testified. They all told the truth as they knew it. Olausen really was a good kid who had spun out of control. He had lots of good friends who were solid citizens and a loyal, loving family.

The result was a new sentence for Olausen: life in prison without parole, an escape from death row to a life of grinding oppression. Grinding oppression especially formulated for one of the killers of Officer James Hoff.

Not surprisingly, the influence of members of the Reno Police Department followed Olausen wherever he went. He was the guy with the black cloud hovering above. To this day, members and former members of RPD appear at any hearings that may provide relief to the convict. It has repeatedly been speculated that influential members of the law enforcement community have "reached out to touch" Olausen. Despite the persecution, real or imagined, he has been a boy scout, doing time as best he could.

The sentence of "life without" was a major victory, but one that was not welcomed in the RPD. "It doesn't please those of us who knew Jimmy," said Detective Todd Shipley. "I don't think justice was done in that."

Olausen's family and Mrs. Hall celebrated, but Olausen stayed a convict, albeit, not on death row. Seeing the remainder of his life behind prison walls, he wanted to appeal the sentence, but Mrs. Hall was a realist, and she was especially realistic about the Nevada government's harsh view of cop killers. Her response:

"Why would we want to appeal this? We've had a tremendous victory here."

With the final appeal finally succeeding for Olausen, on March 30, 1989, the looming specter of death that had lasted for nine years and three months finally vanished.

For Wilson, that specter continues unabated.

Chapter 18

THE ROUTINE

The life of the party prior to June 25, 1979 became back number 14801 at Ely State Prison. Lani's escape and few weeks of freedom in 1981 earned him a berth in the maximum-security bucket, and he came to terms with harsh reality as a man. He resorted to the prison's iron pile to beef his five-ten frame up to bodybuilder and strong man stature. That let him carry himself proudly and confidently, chest puffed and shoulders high.

Although his genes came from Polynesia, Native America and Europe, he regarded himself as Native American, even though he would often be perceived as Hispanic. As a prison inmate moving into middle age, he wore onyx black hair short on the sides and top but with strands past his shoulders in back. To visitors he seemed congenial and friendly.

Lani said he felt sold out by his attorney, Don Pope, but a review of the official files suggested that Pope put in more time in defending his client than the other three attorneys. With Pope as his counsel, Lani was the lone defendant who resisted prosecutors who sought a plea of guilty to a kidnapping charge. Lani was the first to stab Jimmy, and he confessed unequivocally to that in his change of plea hearing. That was enough to put him in Dunlap's sights for the death penalty. Pope helped his boyish client dodge that bullet but he would still die in prison. Or, so many a disappointed cop hoped.

After the sentencing, Pope filed papers to substitute out of the case. Still, there was a further hearing. It came in April of 1998. Lani had caused to be filed a petition for a writ of habeas corpus, alleging he should be freed from prison on grounds that he did not get effective assistance of counsel. He complained that Pope did not advise him properly about his appeal rights and that, when Lani entered his guilty plea, Judge Breen misstated certain laws on appeal rights. Judge Breen denied the petition and found that Lani's contentions were "repelled by the record."

Stites, philosophical and with a background that would attune him more to accepting a "life without" sentence after taking part in a killing, believes that he got a harsh sentence because Jimmy was a cop. He had no quick appeals filed on his behalf, but other inmates sensed he was taking too much of a rap. Eventually, Las Vegas attorney Patricia Erickson came to his assistance as a *pro bono public* attorney, that is, an attorney who provides free legal service for the public good.

In the year 2000, Nevada opened a new medium security prison with an operating inmate capacity of eighteen hundred sixteen men. Located outside the small desert town of Indian Springs it bakes in a desert area about fifty miles northwest of Las Vegas. Stites was sent to the sprawling, treeless, all gray concrete High Desert State Prison when it opened, and that gave Ms. Erickson more convenient access to him. The forty-five-minute drive was much better than five hours to ESP.

As it happened, Reno lawyer Richard LeGarza had filed an elaborate petition for a writ of habeas corpus for Stites in 1993, but it languished without being resolved. Ms. Erickson took the matter over in early 1999, made a wide-ranging investigation of her own and supplemented LeGarza's petition.

In her view, both Judge Breen and appointed lawyer Specchio mishandled Stites's case, much to his prejudice. She wrote that the judge incorrectly advised Stites of his appeal rights in the change of plea hearing when he said, "You understand that assuming this plea is freely and voluntarily entered, there is no appeal?" Stites, just eighteen, answered "Yes." Ms. Erickson characterized that as incorrect.

Turning to Specchio she contended he dropped the ball when, without having Stites's informed consent, he declined to file a notice of appeal. "Petitioner Stites had a constitutional right to a direct appeal on all issues that were supported by the record," she wrote for Judge Breen's consideration. That meant that his loss of appeal rights was "involuntary" and should be corrected. At the conclusion of a four-hour hearing on April 25, 2000, Judge Breen disagreed.

He listened patiently to testimony from Mrs. Stites and four of her children, after opening the hearing with a remark that the four killers confronted Jimmy not thinking he was a cop.

"They thought he was a drug dealer," he said, "and the four defendants still murdered him brutally and viciously, showing no mercy." And as to Fred Stites, a difficult life "doesn't make a person less culpable for murder." He went on to conclude that despite the new evidence of Stites's life under a "drinking, abusive father" and how he tried to "shield his mother and siblings from it," the factors offered

283

in mitigation were insufficient to change the sentence imposed in 1979.

Ironically, Judge Breen publicly debunked the myth promoted by the cops that the killers knew they were killing a cop. Breen did not correct the unsupported kidnapping conviction. Had he done so, three of the four would have been entitled to at least a new sentencing. He knew or should have known that there was either no or very little admissible evidence supporting the charge. At the same time, he realized that, under the law and speculation by the cops, there might have been a kidnapping. Only the youngster in the gang had the balls to resist the gang of prosecutors which included four defense lawyers.

The judge also heard from Public Defender Specchio, who had represented Stites in the 1979 proceedings and who, in the twenty years after that, played a part in defending another hundred murder cases.

"He was not a bad kid," Specchio testified. "I've represented a lot of murderers since and a lot before, and he's not that. He just got tied up."

The judge cut no slack. His denial of the petition opened the door for Stites's first appeal to the Nevada Supreme Court.

When interviewed in mid-2001, Stites displayed a quick, easy smile and deep-set, inquisitive eyes under an even brow. He had his brown hair combed straight back in the style of the Thirties, and his well chiseled face evoked Clark Gable looks. He wore white leather gym shoes, faded Levis and a stiffly pressed short-sleeved chambray shirt, which revealed sinewy, tattooed arms. Asked about earning money, he said he had made license plates and worked in a bookbinding shop at the Carson City prison and sewed curtains at Ely, where he also worked as a teacher's aide.

At High Desert, he sorts playing cards that the prison system packages as a way of making money for itself and its inmates. The state's casinos change decks at their card tables every few shuffles. That keeps cheating down, since some gamblers seek illicit advantage by bending card corners or trying to place tiny marks on the cards. To further thwart the cheaters, most of the playing cards are retired while still in new condition. The job of the card sorter is to reassemble and box nearly perfect decks, which are then sold in casino gift shops as souvenirs.

"I make five dollars a case, and it takes about a day and a half," Stites said. That's one hundred and forty-four decks, each containing fifty-two cards plus jokers and blanks used as markers. When he completes a case, he can spend his five-dollar credit in the prison commissary on shoe polish, candy, chewing tobacco and other sundries, but the commissary holds back a commission of 35 percent. The true profit for Stites works out to about thirty cents an hour for the few hours he is allowed to work each week.

He spends the rest of his daylight hours in the dusty prison yard. At the time Stites was interviewed, HDSP had only been open for a year and wasn't fully equipped, so there was little recreation. The facility, he said, was "too new, and there ain't nothing to do." How did he handle it? "I read, watch TV and walk around the yard and kick rocks," he said, a wistful grin crossing his handsome 40-year-old face. "I can't do much about the situation I'm in, so I have to accept it."

That fit the philosophy of the Department of Prisons, which put up a sign in the prison exercise yard reading: "You are in Prison. Get over it." Nearby, a thirteen-foot-high electric fence was wired to send 20,000 volts through the body of any inmate who refused to accept life on the inside.

Stites's time wasn't all for naught, however. He finished high school "in here" and then earned a general studies college certificate. He has maintained little communication with any of his co-defendants. Although he and David Lani had shared a "house" (a two-man cell) in Ely before Stites was transferred to the new facility, Stites distanced himself from his friend Lani and the two others.

"There's no hard feeling between me and any of them, but I don't care about Wilson now," he said. "He was a thug, more or less."

Even so, as Stites saw it, Wilson still had some bearing on his future.

"I don't think they'll let me out until they decide what to do with Wilson," he said.

Chapter 19

LIFE WITHOUT

"There's a lot of things about prison. Sometimes you find peace in here, and it's totally contrary to what you were told it was going to be. You feel like you don't deserve it."

Olausen, gray-headed and forty years old, pronounced those words at Nevada State Prison twenty-one years after being assigned a back number and twelve years after walking away from the rows of antiseptic cells that make up death row.

He began his prison life on death row, was transferred to Nevada's new death row in Ely and went to general population there. He was on the yard where life had new freedoms and dangers. But he played by the rules and avoided both tangling with and becoming entangled with other prisoners. His good behavior, coupled with maintaining steady work, plus his having escaped death row, finally entitled him to a move to a medium security facility. The system rebuffed his request for reassignment for years, but in 1997, with the threat of a new lawsuit, he returned to the antiquated gray stone walls of Nevada State Prison. His friends and family could avoid 306 miles of the Loneliest Highway for their four-hour visit.

He talked of looking out a new window through concertina wire and seeing quail in the snow eating seeds. He talked proudly of having a "high profile" prison job in culinary administration. He had learned to use a computer and he'd gotten halfway through college. It was vast improvement in a world of misery.

His words came in an interview four years after the move. Still the Boy Scout, he had made a niche for himself. He avoided "ganging up" while building a reputation as a mediator. He crossed racial barriers well enough to be at ease in a Black Muslim prayer meeting while not betraying his blue-eyed heritage. When a civilian supervisor in the kitchen got "sideways" with his inmate staff, Steve stepped in to calm the roiled waters. He built bridges of trust throughout the system while avoiding the associations that spawned divides. He earned the trust of all but the affection of none. The only side he had chosen was his own, but it came across as an altruistic one.

"He was a big boy with the guts and savvy to enforce his will," according to one of his visitors.

Although his faith turned warm at times and cold at other times, he stayed in the Mormon religion. He attended at least one service a week in the Carson City prison, and fellow Mormons were among his visitors.

"They tell me I have the largest visiting list in the state," he said with a chuckle in a meeting with lawyers. "My life's as good as it's ever been, but of course in prison it's bad." He smiled wryly. "Now, with focus, it's easier to achieve."

Olausen, his law courses behind him, understood the implications of the felony murder rule, but remained steadfast in his denial of ultimate responsibility. "It's important to show that I'm not guilty of killing anybody," he said. Looking back, he concluded, "I was a follower; I didn't realize I was a follower. I just thought I was a good friend."

After nearly twenty-two years of incarceration behind him, his search for a way out continued, a sentence of "life with." His family retained yet another lawyer to look for the irregularity in the proceedings that would liberate him, perhaps by way of an application for a pardon, perhaps by way of a new argument in federal court.

"My conscience is that I don't want to be here when my mom dies," he said with considerable feeling. "I don't want to be here when my dad dies. All I care about is for me to be there to support them. I'm not there right now and I want to get back."

He went on to say he would "deal with the realities of my life in here" on his own. "I'm looking at it as a physical deformity."

And yet, after all the unsuccessful court skirmishes, "It's fairly obvious that I'm going to be here a long time."

He described living in a "house" in the joint. Sometimes he's in that house alone and at other times with another inmate. He has a small TV set good for reception of Carson City channels, a radio, books and writing materials. He eats prison food supplemented by canteen goodies such as candy bars and Vienna sausage.

After taking classes to overcome his learning disabilities he earned his high school G.E.D. "I just didn't get it," he said of his reading impairments. He turned to the special courses, then English grammar. "Now I can take a college class. I got a B-plus in English 101."

Escaping death row was a major impetus. He voiced appreciation for the attorneys and judges who respectively went to bat for him and ruled in his favor. "I vowed to myself that I was going to be the best person that I could be. I am the peacemaker, as much as I can be in this place."

He conducted a youth program for younger inmates and "tutored people to help them adapt to prison and prepare for life after release."

As his scholastic abilities improved, he completed a series of University of Nevada Reno correspondence courses. He emphasized child psychology in his curriculum, but he said he had taken "a dozen or two" courses, among them political science, computer programing, computer-aided drafting, ground school for pilots, English as a second language and writing.

His scholastic accomplishments include a two-year paralegal certificate and while at Ely he taught other inmates legal principles. "I got pats on the back for stopping frivolous suits from Anne Cathcart,"[8] he said.

His battles on paper made scant progress, however. In 1996, he, Lani and Stites lost another bout before the Nevada Supreme Court. They filed papers contending they should be allowed new appeals because their 1979 attorneys failed to adequately inform them of their appeal rights. That new argument was filed fifteen years too late and

---

[8] Senior Deputy Nevada Attorney General, now deceased.

should have been filed with the district court in Reno, the Supreme Court said. Olausen refiled in Reno, but his argument was rejected in 2000.

He has seen a glimpse of hope from a shift in Nevada's corrections philosophy. Governor Kenny Guinn appointed Jackie Crawford, a woman whose corrections career began in Nebraska in 1968, to head the prison system in May of 2000. She quickly let it be known that she would work to establish rehabilitation programs for releasable convicts. The state, with a population of two million persons, had a state prison roster of inmates numbering ten thousand, about one out of every two hundred residents, the nation's highest ratio. This does not count Nevadans in federal prisons and county jails.

By early 2001, Crawford had a friendly state legislator introduce a bill to advance education, job training and social skill development among inmates. The bill also called for changing the name from Department of Prisons to Department of Corrections. Crawford wanted to shift away from simply warehousing inmates, albeit with no erosion of security. The name change succeeded. Security may have devolved. According to the correctional officers' union, increased violence was the byproduct of the Director's changes, increasing the danger for Hoff's four killers as well as the staff and other inmates.

Wilson did not find relief from the new philosophy. His sentence remained in place, his hopes pinned to a federal appeal, technically an application for a writ of habeas corpus. As of July 19, 1999, the State of Nevada had executed eight death row inmates since the reinstatement of the death penalty.

Olausen had more reason to hope. He had a new location, a job, and, at the time of the interview, he had a cellmate, one he had selected carefully.

"You have to massage the system and other inmates," he said. "Inmates get to talk and size each other up (before becoming cellmates)." He went on to list five criteria he imposed in accepting an inmate in his cell: no homosexuals, no drug users, no gang bangers, no gamblers and no one with a communicable disease.

"He's a tough kid," Olausen said of his cellmate, a youngster expected to spend fifteen years behind bars. "He's already proved himself; he's had a couple of battles."

He had little to say about Tom Wilson, whom he should have rebuffed in 1979. "I'm very angry with Wilson," he said in measured terms. "There are things that can't be told." But on the other hand, he added, "My heart goes out to him. He never had a chance. Once somebody fuels off (gets sexual gratification) on a kid, how do you re-establish it?" He was speaking of Wilson's alleged molestation by a clergyman.

The prison grapevine had put out the word that Wilson had received a settlement from the Catholic Church on his claim of having been molested by a priest while serving as an altar boy. The contention that he should escape the death penalty also rested on the alleged molestation. It came in Wilson's latest and possibly his last legal paper, an application for a writ of habeas corpus. The thrust was simple: the molestation should be found to be an extenuating circumstance to negate the aggravating factors supporting execution.

The theory is straightforward. Boys who are raped hardly ever report the incidents, out of shame and often a sense of guilt. Many develop a belief that they brought it on themselves. They suffer silently and often socialize poorly. They become withdrawn, and many are poor students. Many investigators suspect that much adult male aberrational behavior— wife beating, drug abuse, general violence, and yes more child abuse, is a result of boy rapes.

Data is still being developed, but some researchers believe as many as one out of every five adult males, and perhaps more, suffered abuse as a child. Few of those commit murder, but many of them harbor deep distrust, if not outright hostility, for authority. They are inclined to antisocial behavior. The lore of psychology is that, in most instances, the victim's sense of worth as a human being sustains heavy damage. It is also thought that, given significant counseling, that damage can be repaired, at least in a functional sense.

Wilson, insofar as the record reflects, had no such counseling.

Chapter 20

WILSON ON DEATH ROW

Wilson remains on death row, the clock ticking, all appeals close to being exhausted. Years of living in a private cell on the row and eschewing exercise left him with underdeveloped shoulders, a flat chest and a sagging front porch. His hairline has receded but very little gray has crept into his dark hair.

To the maximum extent possible in his prison setting, he remains a private man, his brooding eyes set deep in a soft face. His forehead, high and bulbous, suggests intelligence, and a seemingly curious darker ring surrounds the irises of his light brown eyes. Since 1979, he has been dressed in the orange jumpsuit that identifies him as a highly-visible death row inmate.

Wilson's death, when and if it comes at the hands of the State of Nevada, will be by lethal injection. When it happens, he will have many visitors—his last.

The Director of Prisons will determine the maximum number of persons who may be present for the execution. The Director shall give preference to those eligible members of representatives of the immediate family of the victim who request to attend the execution.

On a regular visiting day, visitors wishing to see Wilson at ESP must gain admission through the prison's gates, surrender car keys and other items, show identification, submit to a pat-down search, sign in and go to the Visiting Room. There, they wait until a guard escorts the now six-one, two-hundred ten-pound condemned man into the room. They are watched by Visiting Officers, who sit on a stepped-up platform that is surrounded by a half wall that stops about five feet above the floor. The vantage point allows the officers to see the entire visiting room.

The Visiting Officers watch while inmates chat with their families or lovers. They pointedly show no interest in either visitors or the killer known to them as Tom Wilson. In fact, the officers appear to show no interest in any of the small groups at the scattered tables. Some inmates surreptitiously engage in sexual conduct while some others pass drugs. Mostly it's just mom and dad, brother and sister, or wife and kids, playing cards and trying to come up with something to talk about. The inmates exult in any kind of attention while visitors fidget, waiting for the gates to open and free them to the world outside.

Wilson appears in the Visiting Room with an escort. His gait is slightly ponderous but self-assured. He talks, but never really opens up. He keeps his hands mostly slack. It is as though he is trained not to adopt any body posture that suggests closeness or adopt a stance that could be construed as aggressive. He neither crosses his arms over his chest nor leans forward across the table that separates inmates from visitors, not in earnest conversation nor in any display of hostility.

But he's not passive, only still. He had heard through the grapevine there was a book about his crime in progress. In an interview, he remained calm and guardedly communicative. He worked interviewers like a cop questioning suspects, wanting to know what they know, not wanting to tell what he knows. He spoke often but said very little.

His list of visitors has diminished, and hints of paranoia have emerged, such as a belief that his mother died in 1995 due to poor medical treatment and a concern that his brother died under suspicious circumstances.

Wilson, his eyes watering and red and his voice close to breaking, said his mother's death, attributed to cervical cancer at the age of fifty-three, should be investigated. He suggested that there might be liability on the part of the American Cancer Society for using a pain medication that blocked cancer fighting drugs.

Wilson's father, still alive at the turn of the century, had suffered a stroke and was in poor health. Wilson's contact was minimal with his sisters, but he said he had more contact with his remaining brothers.

Although Wilson said he worked out a lot and stayed in shape by running, only his thick forearms supported that statement. His biceps seemed underdeveloped and his middle flabby.

He is the longest surviving condemned man in Nevada.

In 2017, Wilson remains on death row with some hope that the federal appeals system will spare his life. He has outlived Jimmy's mother. His prosecutor, Cal Dunlap, wondered what good would come of his possible execution. "I don't know if it really means a lot if it is meted out twenty years later," he told news reporters earlier. "For the criminal justice system to have a deterrent effect, the punishment has to be swift and certain."

Very hollow words for Wilson, whose only certainty was incarceration. And arguably, very hollow words for society.

Chapter 21

THE MEMORIES

Jimmy, ever popular with his fellow officers, will be remembered forever in Nevada's law enforcement community. As early as 1982, the first Jimmy Hoff Memorial Awards for Victims Assistance were presented to two workers in the D.A.'s office. A benefit golf tournament and a scholarship fund also bore his name. In addition, in 1987, a police honor guard conducted ceremonies in tribute to Jimmy at his grave on the eighth anniversary of his death.

"It's really nice that they remember," Jimmy's mother Lucille, one of the family members present, said at the time. "A lot of people don't. It's nice that they're having this."

Jimmy was "an honorable man" who "never compromised himself," Officer Gary Eubanks told the estimated one hundred persons on hand. "When you walk your children in the park without fear, think of Jimmy," he said. "Jimmy was one man in a world populated by millions, but if by some chance and hope, there were more human beings like Jimmy Hoff, this world, this society, would be a much better place."

Another eulogist, Sergeant Reavis, said that even in the toughest circumstances, "Jimmy had the uncanny ability of being able to display care, compassion and concern."

Afterward, the officers and family members who gathered at the grave heard a single trumpet play *Taps* as the honor guard stood at attention.

The identity of one person who has honored Jimmy each year has never been learned. "Jimmy's favorite flower was a yellow rose," his Aunt Jewel said. "On Memorial Day every year, there's one yellow rose on his grave. I always put something yellow there myself, but we've never found out who it is that places the yellow rose."

Also in 1987, Washoe County Deputy Sheriff Dick Hintz had conceived of and launched the effort to build a peace officers memorial, even though he wasn't a buddy of Jimmy's.

Hintz's idea caught on. Help came from concerned law enforcement officers and their organizations. They formed a committee to raise money. Among the groups that joined the effort were the Sparks Police Protective Association, headed at the time by Detective Torres, the Reno Police Protective Officers Association, the Washoe County Sheriff's Department and the Nevada Highway Patrol. Jimmy's death was so personal that it drove Torres to serve as chairman of the board of directors for the memorial. Dick Gammick, Jimmy's former canine corps buddy, came on as a member of the board. Still, it was Hintz who launched the drive for the memorial.

"It came together, just people contributing," Torres said. This was the first in the state."

The effort initially generated forty thousand dollars in private donations. That permitted establishment of the James D. Hoff Peace Officers Memorial. By 1990, another twenty-five thousand dollars in donations had been received and included one thousand dollars from former U.S. President Ronald Reagan. The group built the memorial in Idlewild Park, less than a mile from where Jimmy died fighting crime.

The memorial started as a single white stone wall at the south end of the park's Rose Garden. The centerpiece was Jimmy's "block," an altar-like bench supporting the bronze tablet on which an epitaph was cast in bold relief. Beside the words, also in relief, was

Jimmy's portrait, that of a smiling young man with a beard and clean handsome features.

Jimmy's mother, Lucille George, placed a wreath in front of her son's block in the 1988 dedication, and later she turned to Torres and told him, "Frank, this is still as tough today as it was the day it happened."

In 1996, the Sierra Job Corps Center added two more walls.

"Jimmy Hoff and I grew up together as kids...it's a personal thing with me," Police Detective Frank Torres said at the 1996 ceremony.

Lucille died in 1997, soon after the annual ceremony. Since that time, her sister Jewel has filled in. "I've never missed one," she said. Since the day my sister passed away I've put the wreath in front of the block."

In May of each year since erection of the white stone wall, somber law enforcement officers have gathered to affix more engraved plaques to the memorial's white stone walls. Each of the plaques bore the name of a Nevada officer who died in the line of duty. The plaques accumulate at a rate of about half a dozen a year, some from current years and some from years before, all the way back to 1866. Some died in shootouts, others in crashes. Another was directing traffic when a car ran over him.

In the year 2000 five names were added in the annual induction ceremony. It opened with a flyover by a Washoe County Sheriff's helicopter. An honor guard saluted each of the five men, all in the presence of hundreds of uniformed officers standing at rigid attention. Others saluted from horseback and motorcycles as each plaque was uncovered. The haunting, funeral lament of bagpipes that played *Amazing Grace* set the emotional tenor, and a twenty-one-gun salute and *Taps* told of bravery, honor and death.

Speakers over the years have included congressmen, governors, police chiefs, sheriffs and an Air Force chief master sergeant. In many instances, strong emotions about the officers who had given all for a peaceful society surfaced. In others, the speakers stayed strong and stoic. All honored the sacrifices of the inductees, characterized by former Governor Bob Miller as "true heroes, dedicated to law enforcement."

At the start of the millennium, a tan and green cast marker about four feet long and three feet high marked the memorial, with this legend: "James D. Hoff Peace Officers Memorial." That marker sat in a sweeping lawn just north of the memorial's parking lot. The memorial has a rough hexagon shape, with three sides being the white stone walls, one already filled with bronze plaques. The three white stone walls, each about twenty feet long and five feet high, sit atop a waist-high foundation of river rock. Similar foundations reach out like wings to close the hexagonal area enclosing Jimmy's block. The sixth side is open to permit entrance. Finally, at each side, stands a flagpole: one for the U.S. flag and one for Nevada's flag. Tall pines and majestic maples embrace the memorial from the back, and in the distance the Sierra looms.

The epitaph is on the following page.

JAMES D. HOFF
7/17/72 – 6/25/79 [9]

IN JUNE OF 1979 JAMES D. HOFF PAID THE ULTIMATE PRICE AS A PEACE OFFICER. "JIMMY," AS HE WAS KNOWN BY HIS FAMILY AND FRIENDS, WAS KILLED DURING AN UNDERCOVER NARCOTICS TRANSACTION LESS THAN ONE MILE FROM THIS MEMORIAL. JIMMY WAS 32 YEARS OF AGE AT THE TIME OF HIS DEATH.

JIMMY WAS BORN IN WEST VIRGINIA AND RAISED IN SPARKS, NEVADA. AFTER SPENDING HIS TEEN YEARS IN SACRAMENTO, HE SERVED IN THE ARMED FORCES. JIMMY RETURNED TO RENO AND JOINED THE RENO POLICE DEPARTMENT IN 1972. HE SERVED IN THE PATROL DIVISION, CANINE DIVISION AND THE NARCOTICS DIVISION.

THIS MEMORIAL IS DEDICATED TO THOSE PEACE OFFICERS WHO DIED IN THE LINE OF DUTY WHILE PROTECTING THE LIVES AND PROPERTY OF THE CITIZENS THEY WERE SWORN TO SERVE.

---

[9] Dates of Hoff's tenure in the Reno Police Department.

EPILOGUE

Wilson is still facing execution, his very life being the currency with which he will pay for his crime—a crime against organized society, and more particularly, a crime against that society's protectors and enforcers. Olausen can only wait, tears sliding down his cheeks as they often do as he dwells again, again and again on the fact that his bid for parole would be delayed as long as was institutionally possible. Stites and Lani live daily with the knowledge that they face the same delay. Their lives are being paid out, not in the gas chamber but in a cell, each of those lives being drained away from them one weary, agonizing, gray-stone minute after the next, stretching out from 1979 until death in a number of some thirty million of those minutes. Such was the price of a foolish, drug-fogged and deadly teenage bid for glamour, thrills and big bucks.

As heralded as Jimmy Hoff remains, his death casts a long and dark shadow over the department that was supposed to have his back.

After the trial, his survivors filed a civil lawsuit against the maker of the listening device that had been planted under the seat of the 280ZX. That action, Hoff v. AIDS, alleged that the manufacturer negligently caused Jimmy's death by marketing an unreliable device in a setting where it was foreseeable that failure could lead to injury and death.

That suit was doomed to fail. Eubanks had testified before the three judges in the penalty hearing that the surveillance team checked the listening device and that it was working when Jimmy left police headquarters. His statements ran parallel to the grand jury testimony that the device failed to transmit the conversation between Jimmy and Wilson while they were tripping. However, there also was also the previous testimony that the batteries powering the device failed. That, of course, could not be blamed on the wire. Moreover, the device itself "disappeared" and could not be tested or examined for the civil case.

In addition, the tape recording of the wire's transmission had also "disappeared" and could not be examined. Was the disappearance of the tape related to the recording of Olausen's confession? Or, were all the irregularities indicative of a conspiracy to conceal police misconduct?

In response to those transgressions by those who should have known better, Frank Torres reconsidered his decision to leave undercover work. Upon reflection about the deaths of his friends Jimmy Hoff and Ron Chelius, killed within months of each other while working undercover, he concluded that while his departure had been "therapeutic," he had to rejoin the force. "This was a job I needed to do," he said. "Both of the guys were killed because of mistakes, not because the guy was better than they were. Both Ron and Jimmy were killed because of just poor planning and making the wrong mistakes."

Here's hoping he can make a difference.

Made in the USA
San Bernardino, CA
26 June 2017